George C. Needham

The Jewish Tabernacle and Priesthood

George C. Needham

The Jewish Tabernacle and Priesthood

ISBN/EAN: 9783743315112

Manufactured in Europe, USA, Canada, Australia, Japa

Cover: Foto ©Thomas Meinert / pixelio.de

Manufactured and distributed by brebook publishing software
(www.brebook.com)

George C. Needham

The Jewish Tabernacle and Priesthood

THE JEWISH TABERNACLE AND PRIESTHOOD;

A BRIEF EXPOSITION OF THEIR

DESIGN AND TYPICAL SIGNIFICATION. ILLUSTRATED.

BY REV. GEORGE C. NEEDHAM.

As the reader advances with the exposition he will find it profitable to examine the accompanying plates, Pictures of the Tabernacle, its vessels and surroundings, with those of the High Priest in his "linen" robes, and in his "garments of beauty and glory."

In order to have a clear and systematic knowledge of the precious aspects of Divine truth, couched in the types of the Old Testament, it is necessary to have a proper understanding of the type or figure introduced. Some of these types seem fragmentary, scattered along the historical portions of the Word. These fragments must be brought together, that each type may be viewed in its entirety, and present to the mind their proper and symmetrical form. By reference, allusion, comparison, or contrast, the antitypical parallel will be discovered. In this department of investigation one needs the presence of God's Holy Spirit to produce soberness of judgment, and perseverance in a careful comparison of type and antitype.

Frequently types have but one story to relate; one feature of the Gospel to portray; one prominent thought to furnish; one doctrinal truth to unfold. When strained beyond their proper design, erroneous conclusions will be reached. Mere speculation on their meaning, without clear warrant from the Word, will lead to heresy and confusion.

The application of the brazen serpent, and its virtue in healing the bitten Israelites, is applied to Christ as the Saviour from sin. We need not, therefore, speculate on its illustrative teaching, as now we understand its proper application. Thus we are warranted to use those symbols, to which the Spirit calls attention in that inspired Word of Scripture which is "profitable for doctrine, for conviction, for correction, for discipline which is in righteousness: that the man of God may be complete, thoroughly furnished unto every good work."

Chief among the types, and occupying more space than all others, is the Tabernacle of Israel, with its vessels, priests, services, and worship. It is not one type, illustrating one phase of Gospel truth, but many types in one symmetrical whole, expressing the full Gospel of Christ, even the Gospel of our Salvation. Like the kaleidoscope, exhibiting its multiplied colors, and filling the eye with its ever-varying beauties, is the subject of this article. The Tabernacle, to the eye of faith, displays the hidden riches of Christ, portrays His manifold glories, illustrates the excellencies and characteristics of His Person, and points to the accomplished work of Redemption effected upon the cross. The Tabernacle, in its typical signification, occupies a wide range of truth, and is a fruitful theme of meditation. It is my purpose, however, in the present exposition, to confine myself to those parts of the Tabernacle which unfold two great foundation truths, viz: The Person and Work of the Lord Jesus Christ. And heartily do I wish my reader to be saved from idle curiosity, or a mere intellectual appreciation of these things. I earnestly seek your spiritual profit, and the glory of God in your salvation and sanctification.

MATERIAL CONSTRUCTION.

The superstructure of the Tabernacle proper consisted of forty-eight boards of shittim, or acacia wood, standing erect, in sockets of silver. Twenty of these formed the south wall, twenty the north wall, and eight the west wall. These boards were overlaid with gold. Bars ran through rings on the outside of the boards, and one from end to end through the centre of the boards, thus binding them together, and giving firmness to the whole. (Ex. xxvi. 15-30; xxxvi. 20-34.) The door of entrance was at its eastern end, where five pillars stood upright in silver sockets, and from the top of which hung a beautiful curtain of fine linen, interwoven with colors of blue, purple and scarlet. (Ex. xxvi. 36, 37.)

The length of the Tabernacle was thirty cubits. Its breadth is not so easily ascertained, as two of the boards forming the west wall were placed in the corners in such a position as to ensure strength and firmness. It is generally admitted that the breadth was ten cubits. This building was divided into two rooms, by four pillars, from the top of which was suspended a curtain similar to the one called the door, but having, in addition, figures of the cherubim interwoven with its texture. This curtain was called the vail. (Ex. xxvi. 31-33.) The first room, which was twenty cubits in length, was called "The Holy Place." The second, or inner room, being a square, was called "The Holiest of All," or "Most Holy Place."

In the Holy Place were arranged the Altar of Incense, the Golden Candlestick, and the Table of Shew Bread. In the Most Holy Place was the Ark, Mercy Seat, and Cherubim.

The ceiling and roof of this holy house were composed of curtains and coverings. Those inside, of great richness and beauty. Those outside, of a more enduring character. A full description of these coverings is found in Ex. xxvi. 1-14.

They were arranged in the following order: First, the fine linen curtains, figured with cherubim, and ornamented with gold, and brilliant colors of blue, purple and scarlet. These formed the ceiling. Next over them were curtains of goats' hair. Over these were coverings of rams' skins, dyed red, and badgers' skins, which were more for protection than beauty.

The Tabernacle was surrounded by a court—a double square one hundred cubits in length and fifty in width. This court was formed by pillars, standing erect in sockets of brass. (Ex. xxvii. 9-18.) There were twenty on the south side, twenty on the north, and ten each on the east and west ends. The pillars were ornamented on the tops with silver chapiters and hooks. From these depended linen curtains, which went all around the court, forming a wall or fence. It is supposed that these curtains were of open network, affording the worshippers outside an opportunity of witnessing the transactions transpiring within the enclosure. I am inclined to think a more durable and closely-woven fabric was needed. The gate of the court was the proper place for worshippers to assemble. The hangings of the gate at the eastern side were similar to the door of the Tabernacle, being embroidered with blue, purple and scarlet threads.

Within this enclosure were two prominent objects besides the Tabernacle. The Brazen Altar, standing near the gate of the court, and between it and the door of the Tabernacle the Brazen Laver.

The Brazen Altar stood fronting the gate of the court, between it and the Tabernacle. It was made of the shittim, or acacia wood, and covered with plates of brass. It was five cubits long, five cubits broad, and three cubits high. (Ex. xxvii. 1-8; xxxviii. 1-7.) There were horns on the four corners, and a network of brass within the hollow enclosure, forming a foundation for the fire, on which the sacrifices were laid. This was the grate of the altar. There were rings placed on its sides through which staves were passed. Animals were constantly burned on this altar for sacrifice, and its fire was never suffered to go out. When the Israelites journeyed, the fire was probably placed in a fire-pan, or preserved in some other way. A purple cloth was then spread on top of the altar, on which the bowls, basins, flesh-hooks, shovels, and other utensils accompanying it, were placed. Over all was thrown a covering of badger skins, and thus it was conveyed from place to place, the staves resting on the shoulders of men appointed for that purpose.

The Brazen Laver is the next object within the court, and is supposed to have stood midway between the altar and the door of the Tabernacle. (Ex. xl. 7.) As its object was to hold pure water, that the priests may wash thereat before entering the sanctuary, perhaps it was nearer the door of the Tabernacle. (Ex. xxx 17-21.) Neither the form nor size of the vessel is given, but its material was brass, having been made out of the brazen mirrors, or looking-glasses of the Jewish women, which they, in self-denial, but voluntarily, gave as their offering to the house of the Lord. (Ex. xxxviii. 8.)

THE ENCAMPMENT.

We now look outside the court, east, west, north, south, and view, spreading abroad in every direction, the encampment of Israel. It was square in form. The first line of tents were those of the Levites. That tribe was chosen for the special services of the Tabernacle, and from this tribe was the family of Priests appointed. The tents of the Priests were pitched before the gate, at the east side, and at a considerable distance from it. Here also was the tent of Moses. (Numb. iii. 38.) On the south side were the tents of the Kohathites, one branch of the Levite tribe. They had charge of all the furniture; the Ark, Altar, Table of Shew Bread, Golden Candlestick, Laver, etc. These they brought on their shoulders. (Numb. iii. 31.) On the north side were pitched the tents of the Merarites, who had charge of the heavy framework, pillars, bars, sockets, etc. To convey all this material, they were allowed four wagons, drawn by eight oxen. (Numb. iii. 36, etc.) On the west side were the tents of the Gershonites. Their charge included all the curtains, coverings, vails, and hangings of the court. They were allowed two wagons, drawn by four horses, for conveying them. (Numb. iii. 24, etc.; vii. 6-10.) Thus the tribe of Levi furnished 8580 males above the age of thirty, who were the guardians of the Holy Tent and its appurtenances; ministers of the sanctuary (Numb. iv. 47, 48); assisting the priests in their sacred duties (Numb. iii. 9); laborers to take apart or erect the Tabernacle (Numb. i. 51), or transport it across the untravelled desert. (Numb. iv.)

Still further outside the Levitical line of tents, stretching into the distance on either side, were the tents of the twelve tribes. When Levi was chosen to be relatively near the Lord in this service, the tribe of Joseph was divided into two, called after the names of his sons, Ephraim and Manasseh. Thus there were twelve tribes as before. These tribes were formed into four large companies, each company embracing three tribes, with their chiefs, captains, and standards.

On the east was the camp of Judah, comprising the tribes of Judah, Issachar and Zebulun. (Numb. ii. 2-10.) The camp of Reuben occupied the south. This included the tribes of Reuben, Simeon, and Gad. (Numb. ii. 10-17.) On the east lay the tents of Ephraim's camp, which was composed of the three tribes of Ephraim, Benjamin and Manasseh. (Numb. ii. 18-28.) The tribes of Dan, Naphtali, and Asher, formed the camp of Dan, and pitched their tents at the north side. (Numb. ii. 25-29.) There were, therefore, four great camps, one on each side of the Tabernacle, including in their population 603,550 adult males, who constituted the standing army of Israel.

THE CLOUD.

When the Tabernacle was first reared, according to the commandment of the Lord, the pillar of cloud rested upon it, "and the cloud was on it by night and by day, in the sight of all Israel." This cloud, which assumed a pillar-like shape,

Plate 1

THE TABERNACLE IN THE WILDERNESS.

resting on the Tabernacle, spread over the heavens above it, and covered the whole encampment, thus sheltering it from the scorching rays of the desert sun. (Ps. cv. 39.) At night it became brilliantly illuminated, as a cloud of fire, to give light by night to the people. (Numb. ix. 15-23.)

I have now given my reader a brief description of the type itself—the Tabernacle of Israel in the wilderness. We have looked at its external form and internal arrangements. It must have been a stirring sight to have looked upon it really. To have gazed from the top of some near mountain, and noticed the camps, tribes, and companies, with their ensigns, banners, and colors; the squares, avenues, and divisions; the Levitical tents, Court, smoking Altar, and Tabernacle, with its Cloud of brightness, might well stir the heart of the beholder.

When Balaam, the wicked prophet, looked upon this scene, he exclaimed: "How goodly are thy tents, O Jacob! and thy tabernacles, O Israel! As the valleys are they spread forth by the rivers' side, as the trees of lign-aloes which the Lord hath created, and as cedar trees beside the waters." (Numb. xxiv. 5, 6.) There is material enough at hand to produce a more vivid and extended description of this great scene, but enough has been said to suit our present purpose. My object is to present an outline of its general features, and call attention to those truths typically signified therein.

When Jehovah revealed to the people, through Moses, that He desired a sanctuary, to dwell amongst them, they came forward with their voluntary offerings, possessed with an ardor and enthusiasm rarely, if ever, equalled, until Moses restrained the people from giving. (Ex. xxv. 1-9; xxxv. 4-9, 20-30.) The chief metals employed were gold, silver, and brass, of which there were abundance amongst them. The following is a rough calculation of the value of those metals: Gold, $930,000.00; silver, $710,000.00; brass, $1,650.00. Besides this, there were the precious stones brought by the princes of the people, which were employed for the shoulder-stones and breastplate of the High Priest; the linen fabrics spun by willing-hearted women; the acacia wood employed for the structure of the building, the pillars, and parts of the furniture, and skins for coverings. The whole cost, including the workmanship, which was rendered voluntarily likewise, could not be less than $1,500,000.00. Thus we have an example of the liberality of the pilgrim Israelites, when appealed to for means to build a house for the Lord. Gifts from rich and poor were alike received and appreciated.

The principle inculcated in the New Testament, and enforced upon believers of this present dispensation, is that of voluntary giving. (1 Cor. xvi. 2; 2 Cor. viii. 5-12; ix. 7.) Covetousness is one of the sins which God warns His people against. It ill befits one who receives all from Him, to give grudgingly to His service. But where the heart is right towards God, the liberality of the worshipper will be neither strained nor stinted. A right appreciation of God's character

in giving to us the Son of His Love, and the consciousness of our indebtedness to Him for the gift of salvation, will lead to nobility of spirit in responding to His claims upon us.

God's design to have the Tabernacle built was that He might have a house wherein to dwell in the midst of His people. (Ex. xxv. 9.) He was His own Architect. He exhibited to Moses the heavenly model, after which he should form every part of the building. (Ex. xxv. 9-40; Heb. viii. 5.) It was the Lord's House, and He testified His approval of the building when completed, by filling it with the glory of His presence. (Ex. xl. 33, 34.)

If in Egypt the people met with deliverance, when out, and from Egypt, they met with Him who had become their deliverer, and there they became acquainted with His ways of grace and purposes of mercy. In Egypt Jehovah could not dwell in the midst of His people. They needed not only salvation through the blood of the Lamb from the sword of the Angel, but likewise full deliverance from Egypt's power, and separation from Egypt's associations before He could be to them their God, and they be to Him His people. And this separation to Himself God claims from His spiritual Israel, the Church now. His call is loud and unmistakable—"Come out, and be ye separate, and touch no unclean thing, and I will receive you." Happy indeed are those who obey, "that He may dwell in them, and walk in them."

TYPICAL TEACHING.

"Christ is the Key to the Bible. Of Him God has given us more than sketches; the Word from end to end is full of Him. Therein we have a whole Christ presented to us. Christ in His offices, in His character, in His Person. Christ in His relations to God and man; Christ in His Body, the Church; Christ as giving to God all that God required from man; Christ as bringing to man all that man required from God; Christ as seen in this dispensation in suffering; Christ as seen in the next dispensation in glory; Christ as the first and last; Christ as all, and in all, to His people." To understand the Word, then, we must know Christ. To understand its letter will not suffice; we need to know its spirit; for said Jesus, "the words that I speak unto you, they are spirit and they are life." (John vi. 63.) But knowing Christ, possessed with His Spirit, we become qualified to understand the Word, which otherwise will be to us as the letter which killeth, or the hidden hieroglyph which produces confusion. We may expect then to find much of Christ in the Scriptures which speak of the Tabernacle. He said Himself, "Moses wrote of Me." And again, "Search the Scriptures, for they testify of Me." We read, in Heb. ix. 9, the Tabernacle "was a figure for the time then present," and in ix. 11, 'Christ being come, . . . a greater and more perfect Tabernacle.' He is therefore the Key to the Tabernacle. In this type is found all the leading doctrines of sin and salvation. Every pin and bolt and cost? and socket has its own story to relate of the various dignities of

"Thou art worthy of Redemption,
for thou wast slain."

The Tabernacle is doubtless a type of Heaven and of the Church, but in this short exposition I shall confine myself, as already intimated, to those aspects of it which relate to Christ, in order that we may be led to appreciate His relations to us more fully, and realize, without the shadow of a cloud across the vision of our faith, that "He of God is made unto us wisdom and righteousness and sanctification and redemption," and we are "complete in Him."

Although the Ark was the first vessel commanded to be made, indicating its pre-eminence (Ex. xxv. 10-22), showing how salvation originated with God, and how He comes forth to save and bless man, yet that aspect of salvation which begins with man, leading him step by step until he stands in the immediate presence of God, is the line of thought I wish to pursue in the application of the typical lessons which we may now gather from the Tabernacle and its services.

THE BRAZEN ALTAR.

As already shown, the Brazen Altar stood within the gate of the court, and between it and the sanctuary. It was the first object which met the eye of the worshipper. It stood closely related to all the other vessels and all the Tabernacle services. It was called the "Altar of Burnt-Offering," because the whole burnt-offerings which were offered to the Lord were consumed by fire upon it. (Lev. i. 6-9.) The fat of the sin-offering, and memorials of both the peace-offering and meat-offering were offered upon the same altar. It is called "The Altar," to designate the fact that God had but one altar, to which all sacrificial offerings must be brought. It is called "An Altar Most Holy" (Ex. xxix. 37), having been consecrated to its special uses with the blood of atonement. It was the divinely-appointed place of sacrifice, the pivotal cross of, if I may so say, on which the whole ceremonial worship of Israel balanced. Here we see the worshipper and sacrifice, the offerer and victim, the sinner and substitute. His sin is transferred in a figure by the laying of hands to the head of an innocent animal. The animal is next slain, and then consumed as the holy fire feeds upon its various parts. And the animal died for sin, but not its own. Thus the Brazen Altar served its purpose, viz.: to make reconciliation again. Is not the antitype of the altar that cross of our Lord Jesus Christ? "And, having made peace through the blood of His cross, by Him, to reconcile all things unto Himself, by Him, I say, whether they be things in earth or things in heaven. And you that were sometimes alienated, and enemies in your mind by wicked works, yet now hath He reconciled." Col. i. 20, 21. Clearly, then, the cross was foreshadowed here. What truth is there more vital, more precious, and more important than this, "Christ died for the

ungodly?" (Rom. v. 6.) Substitution is the primary truth of the Gospel. "Christ was made sin for us, who knew no sin, that we might be made the righteousness of God in Him." (2 Cor. v. 21.) As the prophet Isaiah foresaw the Man of Sorrows walking amidst the scoffing Jews, and lifted up from the earth as the sin-bearer, he cried, "Surely He hath borne our griefs and carried our sorrows; He was wounded for our transgressions; He was bruised for our iniquities, and by His stripes we are healed." By the blood of the cross, Jesus, our surety, met all the righteous claims of God's holy throne, having made atonement for our sins. The believer enters into the peace and joy resulting therefrom. By faith he beholds the sufferer bearing away sin, sacrificing His own life to save him from the penalty of the broken law which demanded sin's wages—death. Exhausting the punishment due to our sins by draining the bitter cup of Judgment to its dregs; honoring the law and upholding the righteous government of God, bearing our curse, and sin, and doom, we hear the cry of the Victim—"It is finished," and the kingdom of heaven is opened to all believers. The holy fire fed upon the sacrifice. Mercy rejoices with Justice, and Righteousness with Peace. "God is just, and the justifier of him that believeth in Jesus." Thus in the lesson of the Brazen Altar the Gospel shines with undimmed lustre. It is no cold and silent monument, a memorial of the past, but, instinct with life, it cries like the Baptist, "Behold the Lamb of God, who taketh away the sin of the world." Happy the soul who can appropriately say, "He loved me, and gave Himself for me!" (Gal. ii. 20.) We commend to the reader the following passages of Scripture bearing on this point: 1 Cor. xv. 3; Matt. xx. 28; 1 John iii. 16; Gal. i. 4; 1 Pet. iii. 18; Rom. iv. 25; Isa. liii. 12; Heb. ix. 28; Lev. xvii. 11; Heb. ix. 22; 1 Pet. i. 18, 19; Acts xx. 28; Rom. v. 8-10.

> " Not what I feel or do,
>   Can give me peace with God;
> Not all my prayers and sighs and tears,
>   Can bear my awful load.
>
> " Thy work alone, O Christ,
>   Can ease this weight of sin;
> Thy blood alone, O Lamb of God,
>   Can give me peace within.
>
> " I bless the Christ of God,
>   I rest on love divine;
> And with unfaltering lip and heart,
>   I call this Saviour mine."

THE BRAZEN LAVER.

We now come to notice the Brazen Laver in its typical signification. It stood between the altar and door of the Tabernacle. Its use was to hold water, wherewith the priests cleansed their hands and feet, and with which parts of the sacrifices were washed. Sin is not only guilt needing an atonement—a breach of law needing expiation, as we have seen,

Plate 2

HOLY PLACE, AND MOST HOLY.

but it is also moral defilement, and requires cleansing. To those who would render acceptable worship, purity is essential. Washing the hands and feet from outward defilement is but the symbol. At the Altar we have the great truth of justification foreshown. At the Laver, cleansing, sanctification, preparation for service and worship is the prominent thought. The order of the vessels and their relation to each other is significant. The Altar first, next the Laver. Christ *for us* at the cross is the first part of the Gospel. Christ *in us*, as the consequence, by His spirit and word, is the second part. Both stand connected. The Holy Spirit, through the truth, which has a cleansing power, leads us to the blood which faith applies to the soul. Through constant application of this remedy we are cleansed from daily pollutions. And with purged consciences we become prepared for spiritual worship. The following Scriptures set forth this truth: "Christ also loved the Church, and gave Himself for it, that He might sanctify and cleanse it with THE WASHING OF WATER BY THE WORD." (Eph. v. 25, 26.) "According to His mercy He saved us by THE WASHING OF REGENERATION and the renewing of the Holy Ghost." (Titus iii. 5.) "If we walk in the light as He is in the light we have fellowship one with another, and the blood of Jesus Christ, His Son, CLEANSETH us from all sin." (1 John i. 7.) "Wherewithal shall a young man CLEANSE his way? By taking heed thereto according to thy word." (Ps. cxix. 9.) The Word points out the remedy. The Spirit leads to the remedy. Faith applies the remedy; the remedy itself is "the blood of Jesus Christ." Thus are we "washed in His blood most precious till not a spot remains."

To imagine having attained to a condition of sinlessness, when the blood is no longer needed, is to have "fallen from grace." Against this solemn delusion we affectionately warn our readers. Believers should not sin, but when overtaken, "if we confess our sins, He is faithful and just to forgive us our sins, and to cleanse us from all unrighteousness." Exercising ourselves in the Word will correct our wrong habits, condemn our carnal walk, rectify our judgment, ennoble and purify our thoughts, and exalt Christ by constantly exhibiting Him to the soul. Our holiness is not self-attainment, or self-complaisance. It is Christ. And the exhibition of our holiness is growth into His likeness, from glory to glory. In the mirror of the Word we see Him: by the Spirit of our God are we morally transfigured, and by the application of the blood defilement is removed. Thus, the Spirit, the Word and the Blood agree in work and testimony.

THE TABERNACLE PROPER.

This, as has been already shown, consisted of two rooms, the Holy Place and the Most Holy. It was made of boards of the acacia wood, covered with plates of gold, resting in sockets of silver, and protected with coverings of fine linen, goats' hair and skins of animals. The exterior was not beautiful to look upon, but, within, the brilliancy of the gold, the brightness of the light, the beauty of the curtains, and the fragrance of the incense, must have produced awe, reverence, wonder and admiration in the beholder. Christ, when looked upon in His human nature, as the Son of man only, exhibited no glory to the outward eye. Indeed, the Jews "saw no beauty in Him." "His visage was marred more than any man, and his form than the sons of men." (Isa. lii. 2; liii. 14.) Yet was He the Holy One of God, Elect, Precious of whom the Church sings, "My Beloved is white and ruddy, the chiefest among ten thousand. . . . He is altogether lovely." The eye of faith alone can explore His hidden glories and behold in Him all perfection. The acacia wood, or "incorruptible" wood of His humanity is in close relation to the gold of His Divinity. "We beheld His glory, the glory as of the only begotten of the Father." (John i. 14.) Shining out as the brightness of the sun, His raiment white and glistening, we look upon Him on the holy mount, and hear a heavenly voice saying, "This is My beloved Son in whom I am well pleased; hear ye Him."

> "Oh! could I speak the matchless worth,
> Oh! could I sound the glories forth
>   Which in my Saviour shine,
> I'd soar, and touch the heavenly strings,
> And vie with Gabriel while he sings
>   In notes almost divine.
>
> "I'd sing the character He bears,
> And all the forms of love He wears,
>   Exalted on His throne;
> In loftiest songs of sweetest praise,
> I would, to everlasting days,
>   Make all His glories known."

The Tabernacle was God's dwelling-place, and all who sought His blessing approached Him there by way of sacrifice. He has now no local dwelling-place. In "Christ dwelleth all the fulness of the Godhead bodily." (Col. ii. 10.) Jesus said, "He that hath seen me hath seen the Father." God is in Christ, the true Tabernacle, and all who come to God must come to Him through Christ. "No man cometh unto the Father but by me." (John xiv. 6; vi. 37.) Those who speak of the Fatherhood of God, yet reject Christ as the One in whom Fatherhood is known, know nothing of the teaching contained in these types. It is a solemn matter to disbelieve any part of God's truth, and to ignore this great foundation doctrine is a solemn responsibility. "God was in Christ reconciling the world to Himself" (2 Cor. v. 19.) "I in them and THOU IN ME." (John xvii. 23.) God dwelt within the curtains of the Tabernacle by a visible symbol only, and was seen by the High Priest once a year. In contrast to this we can, by faith, always behold the reality of God's glory in the face of Jesus Christ, who is pre-eminently "the true Tabernacle which God pitched, and not man"—the real habitation in whom He dwelleth.

Having entered the Tabernacle, we now stand in the Holy Place. At the east and west ends are two beautiful curtains, called the door and vail. There was but one mode of entrance into the court, namely, through the gate; one way into the Holy Place, through the door, and one way into the Holiest of All, through the vail. "Jesus died the just for the unjust, that He might bring us to God." There is but one way into His presence. The gate, door and vail represent Christ. (John x. 9; Heb. x. 19, 20.)

THE GOLDEN ALTAR.

Facing the beautiful vail, and near to it, midway between the north and south walls, was the Golden Altar, or Altar of Incense. (Ex. xxx. 1–10.) It was a very important vessel of ministry. Though made of wood, it was covered with plates of gold. Its use was to burn incense upon. "And Aaron shall burn thereon sweet incense every morning; when he dresseth the lamps he shall burn incense upon it." This incense was made of four sweet spices. (Ex. xxx. 34, 35.) The fragrance and sweetness of these ingredients were not known till submitted to the action of fire. Hence the phrase, "to burn incense." As the Priest was doing this constantly, it was called "a perpetual incense before the Lord." (Ex. xxx. 8.) To burn incense was a symbol of prayer and thanksgiving. "Lord, I cry unto Thee, make haste unto me; give ear unto my voice when I cry unto Thee. Let my prayer be set forth before Thee as incense, and the lifting up of my hands as the evening sacrifice." (Ps. cxli. 1, 2.) In Rev. v. 8, we read, "The four beasts (living creatures) and four-and-twenty elders fell down before the Lamb, having every one of them harps, and golden vials full of odors (incense), which are the prayers of saints." The incense was offered on the Golden Altar. Of what, then, was it a type? Of Jesus. Prayer and praise is acceptable only when offered in His name. "Whatsoever ye shall ask the Father in My name, He will give it you." (John xvi. 23.) It is He that gives efficacy and value to our offerings of praise and thanksgiving. The Altar was consecrated with blood, and the incense was offered from a blood-sprinkled basis. (Ex. xxx. 10.) The ministry of the Altar was thus closely connected with atonement by blood. And is it not the meritorious sacrifice of Christ which forms the foundation of all true worship, and by which even the sins of our holy things are purged away?

The Golden Altar in the Holy Place reminds us of the scene of our Lord's present ministry. The Brazen Altar outside suggests the work accomplished on earth. But now His work is carried on in heaven, where "He appears in the presence of God for us." (Heb. vii. 25; Rom. viii. 34.)

In Luke i. we read that "the whole multitude were praying without at the time of incense." This is now the believers' hour of prayer, while Jesus intercedes. (Eph. vi. 18; Col. iv. 2; Rom. xv. 12.) A precious thought is given us in Rev. viii. 3, 4. "An Angel came and stood at the Altar, having a

golden censer, and there was given unto him much incense, that he should offer it with the prayers of all saints. And the smoke of the incense with the prayers of the saints ascended up before God, out of the Angel's hand." Thus it is that Jesus purifies our prayers, offering up with them the sweet incense of his own merits, securing their acceptance. How important, then, that our worship should be rendered to God in and through Christ. "No man cometh unto the Father but by Me." (John xiv. 6.)

> "Depend on Him, thou canst not fall;
> Make all thy wants and wishes known;
> Fear not, His merits must prevail;
> Ask what thou wilt, it shall be done."

When journeying, the Golden Altar had first spread over it a cloth of blue, and was next covered with a covering of badgers' skins. It was borne on the shoulders of the Kohathites, with staves prepared for that purpose.

THE TABLE OF SHEW BREAD.

In the next place we come to examine the Shew Bread Table. It stood near the north wall, in the Holy Place. Its material was the same as that of the Golden Altar. It was supplied with smaller vessels, made of pure gold. "Thou shalt make the dishes thereof, and spoons thereof, and covers thereof, and bowls thereof, to cover withal; of pure gold shalt thou make them." In Lev. xxiv. 5–9, we observe the design of this Table. Twelve loaves of unleavened bread were placed upon it, and renewed every seventh day. The bread which was removed was eaten by the Priests in the Holy Place.

That there were twelve loaves has, doubtless, reference to the twelve tribes, even as they were represented by the twelve precious stones in the breastplate of the High Priest. Meantime, I believe, as in the case of the other vessels of ministry, the Table and Bread pointed to Christ. The bread was made of fine flour and unleavened. There was no unevenness in the flour, and it was pure. The corn was crushed, and bruised, and baked before it became food for the Priests. Leaven is the emblem of evil, being a corrupt and corrupting thing. (Matt. xvi. 6–12; Mark viii. 15; Luke xii. 1; 1 Cor. v. 6–8; Gal. v. 9.) There was no leaven in Jesus, "no guile found in His mouth." Nor was there unevenness in His character. His flesh is meat indeed. He calls Himself the true Bread, and the living Bread, which, if a man eat, he shall live forever. The bread which He gave was His Flesh. Priests only could feed upon the Shew Bread. Believers now are unto God a Kingdom of Priests, and as such they are invited to draw near. "Eat, O my friends!" "Eat ye that which is good, and let your soul delight itself in fatness." Shall not our prayer be, "Lord, evermore give us this bread."

> "Bread of Heaven,
> Feed us till we want no more."

Plate 3.

1. Brazen Altar. 2. Brazen Laver. 3. Table of Shewbread. 4. Altar of Incense.
5. Golden Candlestick. 6. Ark and Mercy Seat.

THE HOLY VESSELS.

The covering of the Table was a cloth of blue for its vessels, a cloth of scarlet, and an outside covering of badgers' skins.

THE GOLDEN CANDLESTICK.

This costly vessel stood at the south side of the Holy Place, directly facing the shew bread table, and throwing its light upon it. It was made of pure gold. It was all made out of a talent of gold, beaten with hammers until it assumed its proper shape. The seven bowls on tops of the branches were supplied with pure olive oil, which burned continually. (Lev. xxv. 1–5.) It must have been an imposing object in the Holy Place. Graceful in shape, and elaborately ornamented, giving forth its soft brilliant light, and reflecting that light upon itself with dazzling brightness, it was an object of splendor and beauty.

One thought expressed in the candlestick is Christ our Light. The Spirit was given unto Him without measure. He is the true Light. In Him is no darkness at all. Not only was He "the Light of men," but He fills heaven itself with unclouded brightness. "The glory of God did lighten it, and the Lamb is the light thereof." (Rev. xxi. 23.)

In Rev. i. the seven candlesticks are the seven churches. I think it is no speculation to say that the seven-branched lamp-stand in the Holy Place is a type of Christ and the Church. The branches were a part of the candlestick, and were beaten out of it. When Adam had fallen into a deep sleep the Lord took out a rib, and of that rib He builded a woman, which the man recognized as bone of his bone and flesh of his flesh. They were therefore no more twain, but one flesh. The Apostle, in Eph. v. 26–30, shows this to be a type of Christ and the Church. This mystical oneness is also represented by the candlestick. The Church is One with Christ, He is the Head of the Body, and is seen in heaven. But the Body indwelt by the Holy Spirit on the earth is commanded to "shine as lights in the world." (Phil. ii. 15 ; Matt. v. 16.)

The High-Priest kept the lamps of the candlestick supplied with oil constantly. With snuffers he removed the burnt matter, that the light may shine undimmed and unhindered. Thus Christ exercises His priestly care over the Church. He gives the residue of the spirit. He baptizes with the Holy Ghost. He walks amidst the seven-branched lampstand to replenish, renovate and trim the lamps. He is the Light, as well as Priest. He shines into the hearts of His people, that they may shine out in His likeness. "Ye were once darkness, but now are ye light in the Lord; walk as children of light." It is important to heed these injunctions lest our light become darkness. "Awake thou that sleepest, and arise from the dead, and Christ shall give thee light."

Abiding in Jesus as the living Vine, we shall bring forth fruit. Abiding in Him as the True Light, we shall reproduce that light, in all goodness, and righteousness, and truth. To this end, dear believer, let us seek the fulness of the Spirit,

realize our union to Christ, letting His light shine through us, that all may take knowledge of us that we have been with Jesus.

Like the other vessels it had its covering for protection on the journey. "And they shall take a cloth of blue, and cover the candlestick of the light, and his lamps, and his tongs, and his snuff-dishes, and all the oil vessels thereof, wherewith they minister unto it. And they shall put it and all the vessels thereof within a covering of badgers' skins, and shall put it upon a bar." (Numb. iv. 9, 10.)

THE MOST HOLY PLACE.

Having examined the Holy Place, with its vessels of ministry, let us now look within the vail into "the Holiest of All." This sacred place was four-square, and had but one piece of furniture within its walls. The Ark, Mercy-Seat and Cherubim were all one. The Ark was the sacred chest in which was deposited the Table of the Covenant, Aaron's rod that budded, and the golden pot of Manna. The pre-eminence of the Ark and Mercy-Seat we before pointed out. It was the first thing commanded to be made, and the only vessel of the Tabernacle transferred to the temple. The Mercy-Seat was a solid slab of gold, the same length and width as the Ark, and acted as its cover. On the ends of it were the Cherubim, of one piece with the Mercy-Seat, beaten out of the same piece of gold. This was the only seat in the Tabernacle, and it was God's Throne-seat. The Priests were always standing, accomplishing the service of God. Their work under the Jewish dispensation was never completed. But Jesus, when He finished the work of sacrifice, sat down at the right hand of God.

God, then, had a seat in the Tabernacle. Between the Cherubim shone the Shekinah Glory, symbol of His Divine presence. To this seat of Mercy the High-Priest drew near once every year with the blood of the sin-offering, and sprinkled it upon the Mercy-Seat, and before the Mercy-Seat. Then God communed with man, and blest the people. (Ex. xxv. 16–22.) If there were no Mercy-Seat to receive the blood of propitiation, man could not draw near, for the uncovered law would hurl its terrible anathemas at him. Israel had broken its prohibitory requirements. It could therefore only curse. "Cursed is every one that continueth not in all things written in the book of the law to do them." The law is holy and just and good, but it cannot save the transgressor. It can only thunder out its righteous sentence. "It never saved a sinner; if it did, it would be no longer a law. If it is softened and yielded at any point, it were absolutely annulled. If any sin, or any sinner is allowed to pass, where is the justice of punishing any sin, or any sinner. To bend any commandment for the accommodation of a defaulter is to blot out the law. The law, by its very nature, can have no partialities and no compunctions. It never saves those who transgress, and never weeps for those who perish." How then can a sinner be saved? "The wages of sin is death." The penalty of violated law is death. See then on the day of atonement the Priest slaying the goat for a sin-offering. It is the death of an innocent victim, dying as a substitute for the guilty. Behold! the Priest enters within the vail with its blood, and in the presence of Jehovah sprinkles it upon the Mercy-Seat. The voice of the law is hushed. The sentence has been executed, and now mercy rejoices against judgment. "Without shedding of blood, there is no remission;" but God's eye sees the blood and He says, "Your sins and your iniquities will I remember no more."

Dear reader, thus it is that "grace reigns through righteousness unto eternal life through Jesus Christ our Lord." We have sinned, and are condemned already. Jesus Christ came down from heaven, and took our place under the curse of the law. "He was made a curse for us." He died to hush the law's loud thunder, to quench Mount Sinai's flame. The slaying of the goat was repeated yearly, but when Jesus died, the work was fully accomplished and needed never repeating. "By one offering He hath perfected forever them that are sanctified." He entered into heaven with His own blood, and now we are invited to draw near to the Mercy-Seat, "with a true heart in full assurance of faith."

When the men of Bethshemesh looked into the Ark they were slain. (1 Sam. vi. 18-21.) They removed the Mercy-Seat, the covering, with its blood of propitiation, and the law killed them. When Paul looked to the law, it slew him. How solemn then to set aside God's way of pardon and salvation. "By the works of the law there shall no flesh be justified in His sight." But God hath set forth Jesus to be a propitiation, or Mercy-Seat, that through faith in His blood we might be justified from all things. Christ, having met all the claims of law, and the righteous requirements of God's Holy Throne, becomes our Mercy-Seat. "Let us therefore come boldly unto the Throne of Grace, that we may obtain mercy and find grace to help in time of need." (Heb. iv. 16.) "Not by works of righteousness we have done, but according to His mercy He saved us."

Is my reader a Christian? Are you saved through the precious blood of Jesus? Remember, if yet unsaved, the solemn lessons of the Mercy-Seat. You can do nothing to justify yourself. Your own righteousness will not avail. Your good works cannot meet the law's demands. Why then go about establishing a righteousness of your own? Why not submit now to God's righteous way of salvation? The vail is rent. The blood is sprinkled. The way is open. The invitation is, *Come! Come!!* COME!!! Do not delay. "Now is the accepted time. Now is the day of salvation."

"There is a place where Jesus sheds
The oil of gladness on our head;
A place than all besides more sweet;
It is the blood-stained Mercy-Seat."

OUR GREAT HIGH-PRIEST.

Nearly all religions uphold Priesthood as a necessity. It is absolutely indispensable to Christianity. Pagan nations

have corrupted this office, wh... shamefully perverted it from Ritualism likewise has subve... a human Priest in the place of... it is to pardon and absolve—t...

All these and other perv... kindred doctrinal truths, ari... economy of grace. The ordi... perpetuation of Jewish rituali... respect, they are the substan... shadow; the realities which... antitype typified thereby.

The Jewish Priesthood, ser... present, typified Christ the G... of God, who ever liveth to m...

Though the believer is ab... clothed in Divine righteous... Christ; sanctified through th... reconciled to God through H... High-Priest to represent him... without spot or blemish; to... blessing and glory; to rem... contracted in his pilgrimage... him blameless unto His heav...

"The Aaronic Priesthood... these types and shadows spea... in all the perfection of His... preciousness of His Person, an... character, for acceptance by t... having glorified the Father a... all, for whom He became inc...

The import of the title Pri... cludes ministry. It ensures b... be rendered, a victim to be of... therefrom. This was God's a... priest taken from among me... pertaining to God, that he m... for sins." (Heb. v. 1.) The... were natural, moral and leg... Levi, he must be a descenda... blemishes, superfluities, defect... xxi. (7-21.)

As possessed with moral... compassionate (Heb. v. 2), he... by a special call from God. ... a virgin (Lev. xxi. 14), he mu... ness and defilement, and devo...

In these many respects for... the qualifications of the Lo... character. Called of God to... undefiled in His person and c... passion, considerate toward H... self the Church as a virgin,... dowed with all necessary qual...

Plate 4

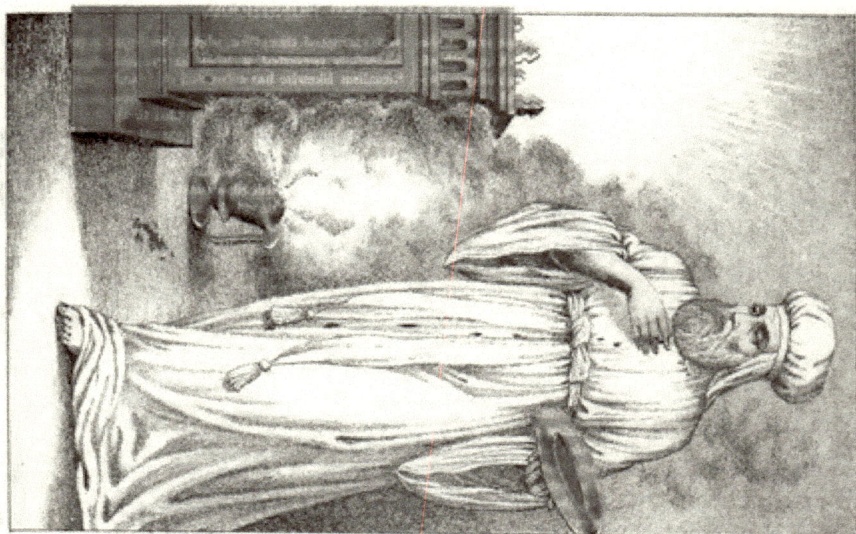

HIGH PRIEST IN "LINEN" ROBES.

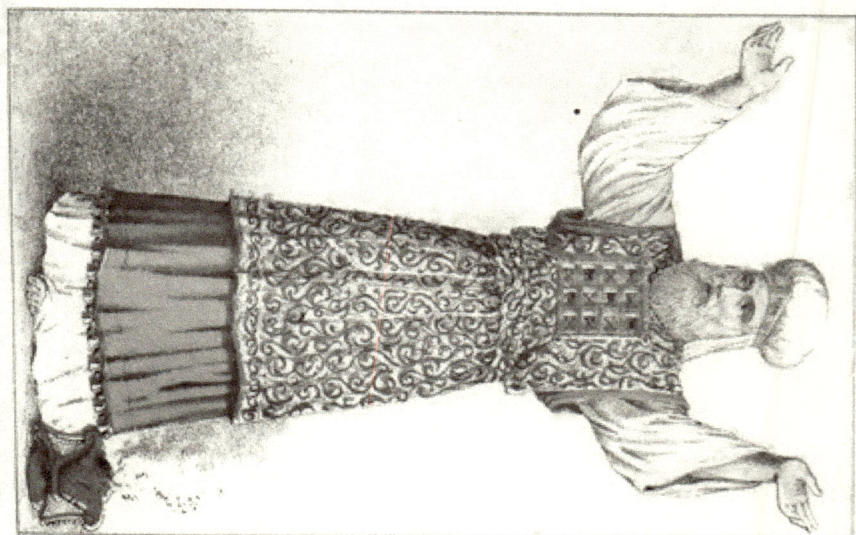

HIGH PRIEST IN "GARMENTS OF BEAUTY AND GLORY."

Having been called and qualified, the Priest's multifarious duties begun. He offered sacrifice, made atonement for sin (Lev. xvi.), offered incense (Lev. xvi. 12, 13), judged evil (Lev. xiii. 2), declared the mind and will of God (Numb. xxvii. 21; Deut. xxvii. 8), decided controversies and solved difficulties (Deut. xvii. 8–12; xix. 17; xxi. 5), represented the nation on the shoulder-stones and breastplate (Ex. xxviii. 9–29), and blest the people in the name of the Lord (Numb. vi. 23.) We observe, then, that offering sacrifice was not the only duty of Israel's Priest. It formed, indeed, the foundation of all other services, and was constantly repeated. It must ever remain present to the mind that "without shedding of blood is no remission," but the remission of sins is only the beginning of priestly blessing.

The present ministry of Christ for His people within the vail is closely connected with the sacrifice of Himself, which, without spot, He offered unto God, as an atonement for sin. He has now entered into the Most Holy Place. (Heb. ix. 9, 12.) He represents His people there (Heb. ix. 24); He offers the fragrant incense of His own merits; He declares the will of God (Heb. i. 1); He rebukes evil (Rev. ii., iii.); He judges our thoughts and ways (Heb. iv. 13), and He returns to bless His saints with an everlasting benediction. (Heb. ix. 28.)

The High-Priest's clothing and their typical signification next claim our attention. In Exodus xxviii. 1–4, and xxxix. 27, 28, we have an enumeration of their several parts. The linen breeches, linen robe and linen girdle may be termed his *personal* clothing. The Ephod, robe of Ephod, girdle of Ephod, Mitre and Crown were his *representative* garments. The linen garments suggest righteousness. Aaron was not personally perfect. The purity attaching to him was derived from his personal clothing. The other garments worn, on special occasions, were "garments of glory and beauty." The light of the onyx stones on the shoulders, and precious stones on the breastplate, together with the golden wire interwoven and brilliant colors blended on their surface, imparted an appearance of beauty which did not belong to him personally. They covered the man; were fitting in every part; were unique in their setting and design, and were graceful to the eye.

By contrast as well as comparison the preciousness of Christ is set forth in type and symbol. Jesus is, in Himself, perfect, covered with a personal glory which belongs not to earth. His indescribable glories are moral, not physical. The unbelieving Jews saw no beauty in Him, but by faith the believer beholds "His glory, the glory as of the only begotten of the Father, full of grace and truth."

The linen coat, which the High-Priest wore daily next his person, must not be confounded with the linen garment worn by Him on the day of Atonement. Both typified the righteousness of the Lord Jesus.

There were two girdles employed; that which bound the embroidered coat to the body, and that known as the curious girdle, connected with the Ephod. The girdle symbolized readiness for service. Israel's Priest was a servant to God, on behalf of the people. Of Christ, it is said, "Righteousness shall be the girdle of His loins, and faithfulness the girdle of His reins." (Isa. xi. 5.) He became servant of all. Girding Himself with a towel, He washed the disciples' feet. (John xiii. 4, 5.) He came "not to be ministered unto, but to minister and give His life a ransom for many." Not only does He wash the sinner from his sins, in His own blood (Rev. i. 5), but as the girded One, He continues His service as High-Priest over God's House. Believers, as priests in association with Jesus, should follow His example, and heed His injunction: "Let your loins be girded about, and your lights burning, and ye yourselves like unto men that wait for the Lord, when He will return from the wedding."

THE BLUE ROBE.

Worn over the fine linen coat was this long, loose garment, called the Robe of the Ephod. It was woven of one piece. There were slits at the sides for the arms to pass through, and a hole at the top, bound around with a strong binding, for the head to pass through. (Ex. xxviii. 31–35.) Around the hem, which descended to the feet, was an ornamental fringe, with tassels depending therefrom, in the form of the pomegranate fruit, and alternating with small bells of pure gold. The color of this robe was all blue. This color was pre-eminent in the Tabernacle and its surroundings. May it not be suggestive of the fact that heavenly ways characterized the Son of God? Blue is the color of the heavens when peaceful and serene. His origin was heavenly. When on earth, in spirit He dwelt there. "The Son of Man which is in heaven." His actions were heavenly. His words falling from those lips, compared to "lilies dropping sweet-smelling myrrh," were words of grace and compassion. They were golden utterances of which we are reminded in the sound given forth by the golden bells attached to this priestly robe. His words of prayer and praise were musical in the ears of His Father. The pomegranate fruit associated with this garment not only indicated the fruitful service of Israel's High-Priest, but His also whom he represented. Fruitful indeed is He in every act of service. By His precious blood a great multitude will be washed from their sins. And if "reconciled to God by the death of His Son, much more, being reconciled, we shall be saved by His life." Because He lives, we shall live also. Thus "He bringeth many sons unto glory."

THE EPHOD.

Over the blue robe this distinctive garment was worn. It was made of fine linen, interwoven with gold wire, and colors of blue, purple and scarlet. It was made of two parts, one for the front, the other for the back, and both were fastened together at the shoulders by the golden clasps which formed the setting for the onyx stones. It was brought together under the armpits by the girdle which bound it to the person. (Ex. xxviii. 6-13 ; xxxix. 2-6.) The onyx stones had engraved upon them the names of the twelve tribes, " six of their names on one stone, and the six names of the rest on the other stone, according to their birth." (Ex. xxviii. 10.) The High-Priest was both representative and burden-bearer of the whole nation. The people were the subjects of his thoughts, and the objects of his intercession. It was his duty to care for them and seek their welfare. In a figure, they rested on the place of strength and security. So Jesus, our great High-Priest, has the government upon His shoulders. (Isa. ix. 6.) But to Him belongs divine might. He is the Mighty God, the Everlasting Father, whose strength never faileth, and whose interest in His redeemed people continueth ever. Securely does He carry them, laying the sheep on His shoulders rejoicing. Herein is comfort for the weak and weary. It is no longer a question of their strength, but of His. They are borne

> " On a shoulder
> Which upholds the government of worlds,"

enfolded in the preciousness and glory of the Great High-Priest.

THE BREASTPLATE.

We shall now consider this beautiful and costly article connected with the Ephod, and made of the same material. (Ex. xxviii. 15-30.) It was woven two spans long and one broad. It was then doubled, to impart strength and firmness in bearing the weight of twelve precious stones. These stones were placed on its surface, in settings of gold, arranged in four rows. All were precious stones, though differing in value and in brilliancy. On the stones were engraved the names of the tribes, each tribe on its own separate stone. The Breastplate was suspended from the onyx stones, and from gold rings in the lower corners it was fastened to gold rings in the Ephod by a lace of blue. Thus it was kept firmly secured over the heart of the High-Priest, and the nation was then doubly represented—upon his shoulders, the seat of strength, and on his heart, the seat of love. What truth is herein signified? Surely, that not only the strength of Christ, the power of Christ, the Almightiness of Christ is exercised to uphold His people, but His affections, His deep, tender, unchangeable love embraces them, holding them ever close to His heart.

In connection with the Breastplate was the Urim and Thummim. It is impossible to tell what these were. The word mean "lights and perfections." Many fanciful speculations have been indulged in by various writers, but it is best not to speculate where God is silent, and restrict our thoughts within the limits of revelation.

THE MITRE.

The mitre, or head-dress, was made of fine white linen. It was the Priest's turban, or head dress. Fastened with a blue rib-

bon to the fore-front was a golden plate, on which was engraved the words, " Holiness to the Lord." (Ex. xxviii. 36-39.) This golden plate was always upon his forehead, " that they may be accepted before the Lord." The nation, composed of individual sinners, was, through God's provisions of grace, represented before Him as " an holy nation, a peculiar people." Such also is the standing of the Church in identification with her Great High-Priest. She is " accepted in the Beloved." There is no holiness inherent in the believer, or wrought out by such, that could stand the scrutiny of God's searching light. But we are in Christ, " who of God is made unto us . . . sanctification." Our holiness is therefore always the same, acceptable unto God ; but it is in the full recognition of this great truth, realizing that He wears for us the holy crown, that we grow in practical conformity to His image, and become gloriously changed into His likeness. Holding loosely our actual standing where God's grace hath placed us, in His Son, will lead either to a careless walk, which disarms our responsibility, or a legal striving for a personal holiness by the works of the flesh, which ignores His grace.

Types speak not only in similarities, but in contrasts also, and in the light of contrast is seen the superiority of Christ's Priesthood above Aaron's. In His personal perfection ; in the value of His sacrifice ; in the scene of His ministry ; in the regal aspect of His Priesthood, typified in Melchizedec ; in the more perfect presentation of the worshipper ; in the deeper discrimination of evil, and in the fuller benediction He imparts, He rises superior to Israel's Priest. " In all things He must have the pre-eminence."

> " He bears the names of all His saints
> Deep on His heart engraved ;
> Attentive to the wants and wants
> Of all His love has saved.
>
> " In Him a holiness complete,
> Light and perfections shine ;
> And wisdom, grace, and glory meet ;
> A Saviour all Divine.
>
> " The blood, which as a Priest He bears
> For sinners, is His own ;
> The incense of His prayer and tears
> Perfumes the holy throne.
>
> " In Him my weary soul has rest,
> Though I am weak and vile ;
> I read my name upon His breast,
> And see the Father smile."

THE COMMON PRIESTS.

Associated with the High-Priest were other Priests, who served under him. Their duties were many and important. They killed the victims ; presented sacrifice ; sprinkled and poured out the blood ; had charge of the Brazen Altar ; saw that the fire was ever burning thereon ; prepared the shewbread ; compounded the incense, and participated generally in the services of the Tabernacle. Besides, they were intrusted with the education of the people, teaching Jacob and Israel the judgments and law of God. (Deut. xxxii. 10.)

Separated unto this work, they were exclusively given to it. From the people they received tithes, which, with portions of the sacrifices and shew-bread, maintained them. When established in the land, fruit, corn, and other produce, according to a systematic arrangement, ministered to their sustenance. Special garments were provided for them, consisting of breeches (Ex. xxviii. 42; xxxix. 28), a coat, or tunic (Ex. xxviii. 4, 39; xxxix. 27), the girdle (Ex. xxviii. 4, 40; xxxix. 29), and the bonnet. (Ex. xxviii. 40.) All these were made of fine linen, and were pure white, except the girdle, which was interwoven with blue, purple and scarlet threads. This dress suggested purity and beauty.

The Lord Jesus Christ is the Great High-Priest; believers (those who through grace have received the message of reconciliation, and are saved through the blood of His cross, joined unto the Lord by one spirit) are identified with Him in His Priestly character, and associated with Him in Priestly duties. "Ye," says the Apostle, when writing to saints, "are a chosen generation, A ROYAL PRIESTHOOD." (1 Pet. ii. 9.) Again: "Ye also, as lively stones, are built up a spiritual house, AN HOLY PRIESTHOOD, to offer up spiritual sacrifices," etc. (1 Pet. ii. 5.) And again: "Unto Him that loved us, and hath washed us from our sins in His own blood, and hath made us Kings and Priests unto His God and Father, to Him be glory and dominion for ever and ever. Amen." (Rev. i. 6; v. 10.)

As none but priests could enter the Tabernacle, so now none but priests can enter into God's presence. The vail is rent, the Holy and Most Holy Places have become one, and those, made priests by faith in Christ, are invited to draw near, to enter into the Holiest by the blood of Jesus, in the full assurance of faith. (Heb. x. 19-22.)

With a beautiful and glorious covering upon us, may we, dear Christian, enjoy our privileges and realise our responsibilities as priests unto God, heeding the injunction, "By Him, therefore, let us offer the sacrifice of praise to God continually, that is, the fruit of our lips, giving thanks to His name. But to do good and to communicate forget not: for with such sacrifices God is well pleased." (Heb. xiii. 15, 16.)

It should be noted, as a matter of vital importance, that the word "Priest," as applied to Christ, or His people, does not imply the continuance of an atoning sacrifice. Atonement has been rendered to God by our Great High-Priest, and His intercession is now based on the ground of its completion. They, therefore, who still insist that ministers, or "the clergy," are priests in the sense that there is a true and real propitiatory sacrifice still offered for sin, trample under foot the blood of the Son of God, and reject the gospel of His grace. " Nor does the word 'priests' denote any particular class in the Christian church. It belonged to Mark, to Phebe, to Lydia, to every Christian in God's church, as well as to St. Paul. Ministerial gifts may and do cause difference of service among

priests." Some are Pastors, some Evangelists, some Teachers, some Helpers; and when those gifted exercise such gifts under the Holy Ghost, their service will minister to the edification of the body of Christ. As regards worship, which is God-ward, all priests, believers, occupy the same ground. There are differences in the intelligence of the worshippers, but the qualification for worship is the same in all—a purged conscience through the blood; the indwelling of the Holy Ghost, and oneness with the High-Priest, who is "now in the presence of God for us."

THE LEVITES.

We before remarked that the tribe of Levi was chosen from the twelve tribes to wait upon the services of the sanctuary. From this tribe was chosen the family of priests, with Aaron as their head. The remainder of the tribe consisted of the three families of Merari, Gershon and Kohath, sons of Levi, who were assistants to the priests in their sacred office. After the redemption of the nation from the bondage and darkness of Egypt, God claimed His right to the first-born sons of Israel to be specially set apart to His service. These would become helpers in the duties of the Tabernacle; but in lieu thereof, according to His infinite wisdom, Jehovah chose the families of the Levites for this purpose. This tribe numbered 22,000 (Numb. iii. 39); the first-born Israelites numbered 22,273; but in order that the proportion should be equal, the excess number of first-born sons (273 in number) were redeemed by permission, at the rate of five shekels each. (Numb. iii. 46-51.) As already stated, about 8000 of the Levites were qualified by age, by physical perfectness and moral qualifications, to enter the duties of their office.

The following extract from W. Brown's book on the Tabernacle, where he speaks on the subject of the Levites, so fully accords with my own view, that I feel I cannot do more to profit the patient reader than subjoining it, as a fitting close to the above exposition:

"The Levites were solemnly set apart to their office by Aaron. Having shaved all their flesh and washed their clothes, they were sprinkled with pure water, and then presented as a national offering to the Lord—the nation's representatives—the elders of the respective tribes—putting their hands upon them, thereby signifying that the people gave them to the Lord in place of the first-born. After being thus transferred to the Lord, two bullocks were offered as sacrifices, the one for a sin-offering and the other for a burnt-offering. (Numb. viii. 5-23.)

"Whatever assistance the priests might require to enable them to overtake their sacred work, the Levites were ever at hand to render it. Sceptics would not be so bold in asserting that it was impossible for Aaron and his sons to do all the work connected with the sacrifices, if they had not wilfully shut their eyes to this fact. It is true the mere Levite could not offer up the sacrifices, sprinkle the blood, burn incense or perform other priestly acts, but in helping to prepare the victims for the altar, and in numerous other ways, he might lawfully assist in the religious services of the Tabernacle.

"In the wilderness the Levites had the sole charge of taking down and putting up the Tabernacle, and of transporting it from one place of encampment to another. (Numb. iv.) At one time the Levites may have been seen busy in the Tabernacle court, waiting on the priests and helping them in their work; at another time, taking down the sacred structure; at another, transporting it and its holy vessels through the wilderness; and at another, rearing it in some new place of encampment; but their duties were not confined to such services as these, for to them, with the priests, the religious instruction of the nation was confided: 'They shall teach Jacob thy judgments and Israel thy law.' (Deut. xxxiii. 10.) These were among the dying words of Moses, and there are numerous passages of Scripture illustrating them, showing that the Levites as well as the priests taught the people. (2 Chron. xvii. 7-9; xx. 19-22.)

"When the children of Israel were settled in the promised land, and the Tabernacle fixed for long periods in the same place, the Levites were relieved of a very burdensome part of their labors, that of transporting the Tabernacle from place to place, so that there was no longer any necessity for them all being in attendance at the house of the Lord, and consequently they were formed into divisions, and waited on the priests in turn.

"When disengaged at the sanctuary, the Levites resided in the Levitical cities, which were situated in all the tribal territories, not however passing their time in mere recreation, but employing it in divers ways for the moral and spiritual welfare of the people. They read and explained the law, assisted the elders in the different towns in the administration of justice, took charge of the cities of refuge, whither those who had sinned through ignorance fled for safety. Dwelling in the midst of every tribe, they were everywhere at hand to explain the law, instruct the ignorant, comfort the afflicted, shield the innocent, punish the guilty, and generally to guide the people in the way they should go. (Deut. xvii. 8-13; xxxiii. 10.) . . .

"Many of the priests and Levites, no doubt, performed their duties to God and man so as to glorify the one and benefit the other, and thereby 'purchased to themselves a good degree.' And having, through the shadows of the old dispensation, led many an Israelite to look to the substance—Christ, the one great sacrifice—they are now among the saints in glory, and shall shine as the stars for ever and ever. Others of the priests and Levites were not distinguished by that holiness which became their office; and at the time of our Saviour's advent, few, very few, were to be found executing the duties of their office with clean hands and a pure heart. But, blessed be God, there were still to be found, even then, some who walked in all the commandments and ordinances of the Lord blameless.

"With all their sins and shortcomings the tribe of Levi,

up to the time of our Saviour, were the custodiers of the Scriptures, which they read and explained in the synagogues, and thus were instrumental in keeping alive, however faintly, a knowledge of the true God, so that, with all their defects, this tribe was of signal service to the nation. By this wise separation of it to God, the light of true religion was kept burning amidst surrounding darkness; the ritual services of the Tabernacle and Temple attended to; and at least a remnant was ever found, even in the worst times, to worship God in the beauty of holiness, and to magnify and declare His great name.

"God has, in the gospel dispensation, made provision for making known His will, instructing His people, and wafting the glad tidings of salvation—not to one nation only, but to all nations, and peoples, and tongues. But He has not seen meet under this, as under the old economy, to choose a particular tribe as His ministering servants in accomplishing these great ends; for while He has given pastors to His Church, He has also appointed all believers New Testament Levites, and separated them from the rest of the world unto Himself. He calls upon them all to dedicate themselves to His service.

"The Levites, when not on duty at the sanctuary, were scattered up and down the whole land, and thus became centres of light from which religious knowledge was diffused; but Christ's followers are scattered through all lands, shining as lights in the world, and by the grace of God hastening on the bright era of the millennium glory when all people will walk and rejoice in the light of Jacob.

"'The beams that shine from Sion hill
Shall lighten ev'ry land.'

"If you have believed in Jesus, and would remain His disciple, you cannot escape His service. He claims you as really as He did the first-born Israelites; nay, He has stronger claims on you than he had on them. He spared them from the stroke of the angel of death, but He died on the cross that you might live for ever.

"Do you then feel the paramount claims He has upon you? Do you count rather than shun His service? And are you often asking, 'Lord, what wouldst thou have me to do?' If so, then you are doubtless already in harness, and aiding on the great work of building up the New Testament Church. Work on, whether in instructing little ones in the Sunday-school, in tract distributions, or in any other way God in His providence has opened up to you. God speed your efforts to advance the kingdom of His dear son. . . . Wherever you are, at home or abroad, in the midst of saints or sinners, at all places and at all times, seek to adorn the doctrine of God our Saviour, by a walk and a conversation becoming the gospel. The Levites, remember, were centres of light! You are also called upon to 'Let your light shine.' 'Arise, shine.' 'Shine ye as lights in the world.'"

FROM

EGYPTIAN BONDAGE TO THE PROMISED LAND.

A NIGHT much to be remembered was that when the Israelites left Egypt. A terrible panic seized the Egyptians when the eldest son was found dead in every house. Under the excitement, the Israelites were allowed to leave the land of bondage, laden with jewels and other articles of value, which they had previously borrowed, or rather asked, and received willingly from their oppressors. Going before them in a miraculous pillar of smoke and flame, God leads them from Rameses to Succoth, thence to Etham, on the edge of the wilderness, and thence to Pi-ha-hiroth, near the shores of the Red Sea. On the third day they are terrified to observe Pharaoh, with an army, chiefly of chariots and chariot-warriors, close upon their rear. Their exact situation cannot be ascertained, but probably they were a few miles south from Suez, shut in by mountains on each side; the Gulf of Suez, some six or eight miles broad, in front, and the Egyptian army behind. The terror and anxiety of the host of Israel are at their height, when slowly and majestically the pillar of cloud and fire that had gone before them moves to their rear, and throws a screen between them and their pursuers. A miraculous power imparted during the night to a strong east wind, causes it to lay bare a passage across the Gulf, wide enough for the whole host to cross. The fiery column sheds its glare before them, and guides them safely to the further shore. Tempted, amid the darkness of night, to follow them, Pharaoh and all his host are caught and overwhelmed in the returning waters. Israel's bondage is over; the oppressor's yoke is broken; the people of the Lord are free.

Alas! a worse yoke is upon the neck of every human being. By nature we are all the children of wrath, and in the thralls of Satan. The world itself is one vast house of bondage, and its different inhabitants the slaves of divers lusts and passions. We are all fallen into captivity and servitude, and Gold, Ambition, Appetite, are the slave-owners. Woful is the bondage where the higher nature is in thraldom to the lower. Christ only can break the yoke and let the oppressed go free. And in the deliverance of Israel the great work of redemption is symbolized, and sinners are pointed to One who can free them from a worse tyrant and taskmaster than Pharaoh and the Egyptians.

It is a fresh April morning. Three millions of people line the shores and crowd the heights on the Sinai side of the Gulf of Suez. Here, at the water-edge, may be seen groups of men and women, watching the rolling tide as it casts heavily on the beach the ghastly corpses of the Egyptian warriors—perhaps stripping them of their rings and necklaces, and the weapons which are yet grasped in their bleached and bloodless hands. Yonder, where the rock juts out into the sea, are clusters of children gathering the rich red sea-weed, or the brilliant shells and corals, or watching the movements of the strange-looking creatures that roam among the pools. Away, dotted over the rocky heights, or in closer masses in the hollows between, are flocks of sheep, goats, oxen and camels, cropping the spare herbage of the desert, or making eager journeys in quest of water. Conspicuous above the encampment, and contrasting strikingly with the clear blue of the April sky, is the strange column that ever rolls up its wreaths of smoke and fire, as if in communication with heaven. An expression of happy freedom seems to sit on every face. One countenance, however, looks as though the spirit of composure and the spirit of anxiety were moulding it by turns. Others may be deeming their troubles past; but that thoughtful, king-like man, with the eagle eye, and the mild expression, and the massive brow, knows that they are but beginning.

Thus the Israelites commenced their wanderings in the wilderness. The Red Sea was behind and a trackless desert before them, but God was their leader, and his cloudy banner floated in the sky, a waving pennant by day, and a flaming torch by night. Under Divine direction they took their course toward Sinai. They first went three days' journey down the eastern shore of the Red Sea, between the coast on the right and the mountainous ridge on the left, until they came to Marah. During this march they suffered fearfully from thirst. Let us not think lightly of their distress. The sensation we call thirst is no more like the mud and raging fever of the desert than our cool and verdant valleys are like the baked and blistering rocks of that burning wilderness. The vast host of men, women and children, with great herds of cattle, had to travel over the sandy waste on foot, with the burning sun over their heads, and their sufferings were horrible. Look the individuals in the face! They plod moodily, heavily on, no man speaking to his fellow. Many cannot speak if they would. Their tongues are parched and rough, and cling to the roofs of their mouths; their lips are black and shrivelled, and their eye-balls are red with heat, and sometimes a dimness comes over them which makes them stagger and fall. Not one in that multitude but would part with limb or life for one cool draught of water.

But, lo! their misery they think is past. In the distance

13

they [...] hold trees and bushes, clad in refreshing green. There must be water near. With glad looks and quickened steps they push joyously on. What a rush to the water—what eagerness to gulp the refreshing flood! Whence that universal groan of horror and despair? The water is *bitter*, so bitter as to be loathsome even to their intense agony of thirst. Pity them; but judge them not too severely, if in that awful moment of disappointment, with the waters of Marah before their faces, and the waters of the Nile before their thoughts, they sorrowed and complained that they had been brought from unfading waters to perish in that thirsty desolation.

Their sin was pardoned, the waters healed, and they passed on to Elim, six miles further, where there were twelve wells of water, and threescore and ten palm trees. Their next encampment was in a valley by the Red Sea, on the edge of the Wilderness of Sin. This wilderness is memorable as the place where, in answer to their murmurings, the Israelites were, for the first time, miraculously fed with quails, to appease their lusting after the flesh-pots of Egypt. Here also they were first fed with manna, which they continued to eat for forty years, until they reached the land of promise, and ate of the corn of that land.

They now entered the Wady Feiran, and penetrated into the inner and most mountainous part of the peninsula. Having halted at Alush and Dophkah, they reached Rephidim, whence Moses went with the Elders to strike the rock in Horeb, and procure from it a supply of water. Tradition points out, as the rock which Moses struck, a large block of granite, some twenty feet in height, marked by several horizontal grooves, like mouths, such as might have been formed by the flowing of water. At Rephidim they encountered and conquered the Amalekites—a tribe of Edomites, fired by the fiercest jealousy, on account of Jacob's seed having been preferred to Esau's, who came upon their rear and annoyed the feeble and helpless of the host. Moses, with his hands supported by Aaron and Hur, held his rod outstretched while this battle was going on, in token of dependence on the help of God. Here also occurred the visit of Jethro, the father-in-law of Moses, and the establishment of subordinate courts of justice, according to his advice.

The next encampment was at Mount Sinai. Here the mountains assume that bold, tall and fearfully bare aspect, which gives to the district its peculiar character of majesty and desolation. No one who has not seen them can conceive the ruggedness of the vast piles of granite rocks, rent into chasms, rounded into small summits, or splintered into countless [...], all in the wildest confusion, as the [...] of an observer from any of the heights. We may imagine what a strange and solemn region it would be to Israel—come away from the Nile, broad and overbrimming, to those [...] down which nothing flowed but rivers of hot air; from [...], fresh [...] and springing [...] of Goshen and Memphis—to the [...] those which seemed to await the voice of the [...] and the [...] lofty peaks which, relieved by no

verdure, and interrupted by no life, carried the eye that rested on them straight up to heaven. If it be the perfection of a place of worship to have nothing to distract the mind, there could be nothing more stern and still than this inland solitude, with its granite pinnacles soaring up nine thousand feet into the firmament—an Alpine skeleton, a Tyrol or Savoy, with its forests and its snows torn off, and its lakes dried up—the ruins of a world.

So awful was the sanctuary, so sublime the pulpit, to which Jehovah led his people, that they might hear his memorable sermon, and receive the statute-book of heaven. Here the law was given. The rules of eternal righteousness, which had been lying about the world, tossing along from age to age, without arrangement and without authority, were handed forth from heaven anew; and clear beyond cavil, sufficiently compact for the smallest memory, and comprehensible by the feeblest understanding, they became to mankind a statute-book forever, direct from the presence of Infinite Majesty, and in the solemnities by which it was sanctioned, suggestive of that awful tribunal when it will reappear as the law by which the righteous Judge shall render to every man according to his deeds.

Here the Tabernacle was set up—a peripatetic shrine, a cathedral that could be carried about, a temple of canvas and tapestry which accompanied Israel in their wanderings, and which sufficed as a visible centre of worship until such time as the waving tapestry solidified into carvings of cedar, and the badger skins were replaced by tall arcades of marble, and the tent had grown to a temple. The worship of the one living and true God there inaugurated now counts its adherents by hundreds of millions, and includes all that is worth naming of the world's intelligence and civilization. All the inhabitants of Europe are monotheists. Save a few savage tribes, and a handful of Pagans from Asia, all the inhabitants of America are monotheists. Every Christian in the world is a monotheist; so is every Jew; so is every Mussulman. To-day one-half the people upon the globe worship the God of Moses.

From Mount Sinai the course of the Israelites was for some distance nearly due north, down a broad valley which descends by a gradual slope from the tangled labyrinth of the Sinaitic group toward the crescent-shaped ridge of mountains, El Tih, which forms the lofty buttress of the great desert. They tarried for some time at Hazeroth, ever memorable by reason of the curious sedition of Miriam and Aaron. In this neighborhood they were miraculously fed with quails for a whole month. From the plain of Hazeroth they ascended one of the passes of the Tih, to the broad plains of the desert above. From this position they must have turned their course in a northeasterly direction, toward the head of the Gulf, or advanced northward across the desert, toward the land of Canaan. The latter route seemed to be distinctly mentioned by Moses in his recapitulation of their march through this great and terrible wilderness, as they came to Kadesh Barnea.

WANDERINGS OF THE ISRAELITES.

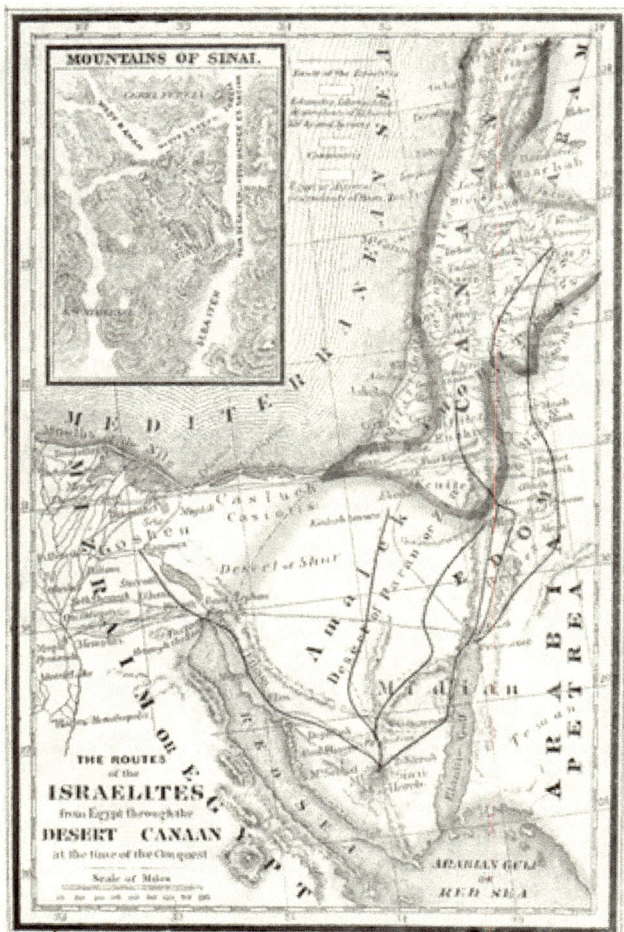

THE ROUTES
of the
ISRAELITES
from Egypt through the
DESERT and CANAAN
at the time of the Conquest

Scale of Miles

EXPLANATION OF MAP.

Dr. Robinson's admirable maps, executed by Kiepert under Dr. Robinson's personal direction, afford the basis on which this and the map of Palestine are constructed. The plains on the south of Sinai are represented in connection with that of Er Rahah, where, according to Dr. Robinson, the Israelites probably stood while the law was given; this is done by simply modifying the plan of the Sinaitic group.

The plain of Sebaiyeh is seen extending several miles on the south and east Sinai, offering a wider range for the hosts of Israel; and this is assumed by Ritter and many others to have been the station of the Israelites when they received the law.

The route and stations of the Israelites are quite conjectural after we leave Sinai. The track of the Israelites, as sketched by Dr. Robinson, is indicated by the continuous red line.

The deviations from this route are indicated by the shorter yellow lines. The deviations are indicated on the supposition that the children of Israel occupied the plains on the south of Sinai, and proceeded toward Beer-sheba in a direct line across the desert to Kadesh-barnea. And after wandering thirty years in the desert, they are found in the deep valley below the Dead Sea, at another Kadesh-barnea. This supposes that there were two places named Kadesh-barnea —one on the western part of the great plateau of the desert, the other below the Red Sea, in the deep valley of Arabah.

It is contended with earnestness and great force by Lepsius, that Mount Serbal, northwest from Sinai a day's journey, near the Desert of Sin, was the place where the law was given. Though inferior in height, Mount Serbal rises in loncher and loftier grandeur to the observer than Sinai itself. About its base, watered by perennial streams, a charming oasis of richest verdure spreads. On its rocky facings are formed mysterious Sinaitic inscriptions—the lingering records of a people whose language, religion and country are totally lost. The probable route of the Israelites through the desert would be changed again by this theory of Lepsius, but we cannot well make Serbal conform to the conditions of the narrative, as it stands without the group of Sinai.

This outpost of Canaan, so remarkable in the history of the Exodus, we locate in the midst of this desert, fifty miles or less south of Beersheba.

Disheartened by the report of the spies, the Israelites murmured and rebelled, and were sentenced to linger and die in the wilderness. Then relenting, they went up to fight with the Amalekites and Canaanites, and were discomfited, "even unto Hormah." From Hormah, at the command of God, they returned toward the east arm of the Red Sea, to wander forty years in the wilderness, until they should be consumed and die there for their rebellion against God. Of their subsequent wanderings for thirty-eight years we know nothing. Eighteen stations are specified as occupied in this interval, but of these nothing is known. The Israelites, like the modern Bedouins, doubtless spent this time in roving up and down the Arabah, and over the vast desert of Paran, between Sinai and Palestine, according as they could find pasturage and water. The rebellion of Korah, Dathan, and Abiram, is referred to this interval, but the date and place of this judgment are alike unknown.

In the first month, April, they again returned to Kadesh, which they had left in the third or fourth month, almost thirty-eight years before. On their return to Kadesh, Miriam dies; the people murmur for water; Moses and Aaron being water from the rocks, but, in doing this, sin against God, and receive sentence of death without seeing that good land beyond Jordan, so long the object of their desire; a passage is demanded through the land of Edom, and is refused. The Israelites then journeyed from Kadesh to Mount Hor, or Mosera, where Aaron died. While in this vicinity, they gained a signal victory over the Canaanites, by whom they had been repulsed on their previous attempt to go up into Palestine.

Mount Hor is a high, rocky peak, in the mountains of Edom, east of the Arabah, and situated midway between the Dead Sea and the Arabah. It rises, in lone majesty, above the surrounding summits, and overlooks a boundless prospect of craggy cliffs, gloomy ravines, and lofty, barren deserts. The grandeur and sublimity of the scene from the summit of Mount Hor is forcibly sketched by Dr. Wilson, in the following paragraph: "After the greatness and peril of the effort which we had been compelled to make, we should, in ordinary circumstances, have been elated with the success which we had experienced; but the wild sublimity and grandeur and terror of the new and wonderful scene around and underneath us, overawed our souls. We were seated on the very throne, as it appeared to us, of desolation. Its own metropolis of broken and shattered and frowning heights—ruin piled upon ruin, and dark and devouring depth added to depth—lay on our right hand and on our left. To the rising sun, Mount Seir, the pride and glory of Edom, and the terror of its adversaries, lay before us—smitten in its length and breadth by the hand of the Almighty stretched out against it—barren and most desolate, with its daughter, the 'city of the rock,' over-

thrown and prostrate at its feet. To the west, we had the great and terrible wilderness, with its deserts and pits and droughts spread out before us, without any land but its own vastness, and pronounced by God himself to be the very 'shadow of death.'" Here Moses took Aaron and Eleazer, and went up into Mount Hor in the sight of all the congregation, where these venerable pilgrims took their last farewell of each other, and "Aaron died there, in the top of the mount." A tomb has been erected to his memory on the summit, which has often been visited and described by modern travellers.

From Mount Hor the Children of Israel passed along the Arabah, south to Ezion-Geber, at the head of the Eastern or Atlantic Gulf, which is several times denominated the Red Sea. Elath and Ezion-Geber were both situated at the head of this gulf. The latter afterward became famous as the port where Solomon, and after him Jehoshaphat, built fleets to carry on a commerce with Ophir. Here they turned eastward, up the pass that leads to the high plain of the great eastern desert of Arabia. At this place a large defile comes down steeply from the northeast through the mountains, forming the main passage out of the great valley to this desert. The ascent of the Israelites was, doubtless, through this pass, when they departed from the Red Sea, and turned north to "compass Edom," and to pass on to Moab, and to the Jordan. It was at this point in their wanderings that "the people were much discouraged because of the way;" and they were bitten by fiery serpents. Burckhardt informs us that this place is still infested by poisonous serpents, which are greatly feared by the inhabitants.

The course of the Israelites now lay along the border of the eastern desert, back of Mount Seir, the Mountains of Edom. The Edomites, who had refused the Children of Israel a passage through their land from Kadesh, now suffered them to pass unmolested along their borders on the east, and even supplied them with provisions for their march. Nothing is known of the places mentioned in the interval until the Israelites arrived at the brook Zered, or Sared, a marshy valley which rises in the eastern desert, near the present route to Mecca, and after a course of several miles to the west, discharges, in the rainy season, its waters through the southeastern shore of the Dead Sea. In the summer season the channel is dry. For some distance from the sea the channel of this brook is, like all similar valleys in this region, a deep and almost impassable gorge. This is the "brook of the wilderness" (Isa. xv. 7); and, according to Ritter, the "river of the wilderness." (Amos vi. 14.) It was the southern boundary of Moab. From this station the Children of Israel passed without molestation around Moab, on the borders of the desert, to the river Arnon, twenty-five or thirty miles farther north. They were now on the borders of the Ammonites, who, like the Moabites, had been reduced so as to retain a mere remnant of their former possessions. They seem, at this time, to have occupied the margin of the desert to the right of the Israelites. This portion of the desert eastward bore the name of Kedemoth.

The children of Israel now encountered a formidable foe in the Amorites, whom they conquered. From the station on the banks of the Arnon to the plains of Moab, on the east of Jordan, opposite Jericho, the accounts of the intervening stations seem to be contradictory. After the conquest of Sihon, the Israelites directed their forces against Og, the giant of Bashan, the capital of whose kingdom was Edrei, fifteen miles east of the northern extremity of the Sea of Galilee, and seventy-five from the plains of Moab. From Bashan the Israelites spread their conquests farther north, over all the region of the Sea of Galilee and the waters of Merom, as far as Mount Lebanon. The Moabites, well pleased with the subjugation of the Amorites, were still the foes of the Israelites. Though fearing to engage with them in open war, they called Balaam from beyond the Euphrates to curse these hated invaders (Numb. xxii., xxiii., xxiv.); but finding no enchantment to prevail against them, they succeeded by wiles, in harmony with their own incestuous origin, in bringing a plague upon the people, by which 24,000 perished. The Israelites lingered four or five months on the plains of Moab, over against Jericho, in full view of their future inheritance. During this time they had subdued their enemies before them, and Moses had written the book of Deuteronomy, recapitulating the blessings and the curses of their law, and recording his final exhortations and entreaties, in the full consciousness that his eventful life was advancing to a close. His last military act was to wage, by God's command, an exterminating war against the Midianites for their agency in enticing the Israelites into sin. In the dreadful carnage of this expedition, Balaam, the apostate prophet, was slain.

And now nothing remained for the great leader to do but to pour out his heart before the people in lofty odes and eloquent blessings, and then ascend the mountain and die. And never does Moses wear such an air of moral sublimity, as when we behold him leaving the camp and his beloved people, and climbing the summit, where, with the rock for his couch and the broad heaven for his roof, and far from all human companionship, he was to submit himself to the sentence: "Dust thou art, and unto dust thou shalt return." We cannot follow Moses in this mysterious journey. If the lawgiver had received a rebuke, this was more than compensated by the peculiar distinction attending his exit. His humiliation only brought out more strikingly his real grandeur. Although the sentence shutting him out from Canaan was not literally reversed, its bitterness was greatly mitigated. From Nebo he looked down on the palm-trees of Jericho, close under his feet; and from the warm valley through which the Jordan was gleaming, far across to yon boundless sea; from Jezreel, with its waving corn, to Eshcol, with its luxuriant vines; from Bashan, with its kine, to Carmel, with its rocks dropping honey; from Lebanon, with its rampart of snow, south again to the dim edge of the desert; and as he feasted his eyes upon the rich landscape of Canaan, its fountains and brooks and olives and vines, as what had so long been the land very far off, and what to the fretful host in the wilderness had seemed no better than a myth or a mirage; as this splendid domain spread out, hill and valley, field and forest, in the bright garb of spring, the Lord said, "This is the land!" "This is the land which I sware unto Abraham and Isaac and Jacob, saying, I will give it to thy seed." But beautiful and overwhelming as it was, just then there began to rise on Moses' sight a still more wondrous scene. It was no longer the Jordan with its palms, but a river of water clear as crystal, and on either side of it a tree of life o'ercanopying. It was no longer Nebo's rocky summit, but a great white throne, and round it light inaccessible, and before him spread out a better land than the land of promise. "So Moses, the servant of the Lord, died." The spirit was gone home. Behind that countenance, still radiant with the beatific vision, no longer worked the busy brain, no longer went and came the mind which so long had conversed with God, and managed the affairs of the chosen people. Powerless is the hand which had swayed Jehovah's rod and split the sea asunder; and cold in its unconsciousness is that majestic presence before which proud Pharaoh learned to tremble. A corpse is all that now remains of the mighty prophet and law-giver, and there is no man there to bury him. But He who preserved his infant body amid the bulrushes, takes charge now of his lifeless remains. Those hands which had taken the law from God, those eyes which had seen His presence, those lips which had conversed with the Almighty, that face which had been irradiated with the beams of heavenly glory, must not be neglected, though the soul is gone. "The Lord buried him in a valley in the land of Moab, over against Bethpeor."

Upon the death of Moses, Joshua, now in his eighty-fifth year, assumed the command of the people, sent spies into Jericho, crossed the Jordan, fortified a camp at Gilgal, circumcised the people, and kept the passover; then pressed forward to the conquest of the Canaanites, and soon was master of the greater part of Palestine. He died at the age of one hundred and ten years, and was buried in his own city, Timnath-serah.

JERUSALEM.

The situation of Jerusalem is very remarkable. It stands upon an upland ridge about 2300 feet above the level of the Mediterranean, and 3500 feet above that of the Dead Sea. The town is surrounded on three sides by steep, rocky ravines, the valley of Jehoshaphat on the east, and the valleys of Gihon and Hinnom on the west and south. These ravines are shaped somewhat like a horse-shoe, the open part being towards the northwest. The city itself, lying within the horse-shoe, spread ultimately over four hills or heights, called Zion, Moriah, Acra, and Bezetha. The chief of these hills was Zion; it lay, so to speak, in the western bend of the horse-shoe. In David's time the whole town lay on its northern slope. Additions were made at subsequent times. Between the hills ran valleys, the chief of which was called by the Romans the Tyropœos; but the seventeen great sieges of Jerusalem have caused many of these valleys to be filled up with rubbish, and internally the city now is very much changed from what it must have been. On all sides the neighboring mountains rise somewhat above the city, verifying the simile of the psalm, "As the mountains are round about Jerusalem, so the Lord is round about His people from henceforth even forever." The most celebrated of the hills that thus environ the sacred city is Mount Olivet. It stretches away to the northeast, in the form of a ridge with several summits, rising to the height of 400 feet above the valley of Jehoshaphat, and 2500 above the level of the Mediterranean. South of Olivet is the Hill of Offense; so called because believed to be that on which Solomon built shrines to Chemosh and Moloch. The Hill of Evil Counsel is opposite Mount Zion, having its name from the circumstance that here, in the country-house of Caiaphas, the priests and elders took counsel to put Jesus to death. Mount Gihon guards the city on the west, and Mount Scopus on the north. The brook Kidron runs, or rather ran, through the valley of Jehoshaphat, passing the Garden of Gethsemane near the road to the Mount of Olives and Bethany.

Mount Zion is far the most conspicuous of the hills on which Jerusalem is built. It rises abruptly to the height of nearly 300 feet from the valley of Hinnom, sloping down more gradually "on the sides of the north," where lay the city of the Great King. It was a place of remarkable strength, so that the tabernacle, the palace of David, and the other buildings that stood on it were remarkably secure. (Ps. xlviii.) Part of the hill is now under regular cultivation; thus verifying Micah's prophecy, that Zion should be "ploughed as a field."

The view of Jerusalem from some of the neighboring heights is apt to disappoint the traveller; but from the Mount of Olives it is exceedingly striking. When seen from that point, the hill of Zion justifies the admiring exclamation of the Psalmist, "Beautiful for situation, the joy of the whole earth, is Mount Zion." Although the size of Jerusalem was not very great, its situation, on the brink of rugged hills, encircled by deep and wild valleys, bounded by eminences whose sides were covered with groves and gardens, added to its numerous towers and temples, must have given it a singular and gloomy magnificence, scarcely possessed by any other city in the world. It is true, the ancient city beloved by God has now disappeared, and with it all the hallowed spots once contained within its walls. Yet the face of nature still endures; the rocks, mountains, lakes and valleys are still unchanged, save that loneliness and wildness are now where once were luxury and every joy; and though their glory is departed, a high and mournful beauty still rests on many of their settled scenes. Amidst them a stranger will ever delight to wander; for there his imagination will seldom be in fault; the naked mountain, the untrodden plain, and the voiceless shore will kindle into life around him, and his every step be filled with those deeds through which guilt and sorrow passed away, and life and immortality were brought to light.

No human being could be disappointed who first saw Jerusalem from the east. The beauty consists in this, that you then burst at once on the two great ravines which cut the city off from the surrounding table-land, and that then only you have a complete view of the Mosque of Omar. The other buildings of Jerusalem which emerge from the mass of gray ruin and white stones are few, and for the most part unattractive. What, however, these fail to effect, is in one instant effected by a glance at the Mosque of Omar. From whatever point that graceful dome, with its beautiful precinct, emerges to view, it at once dignifies the whole city. And when, from Olivet, or from the Governor's house, you see the platform on which it stands, it is a scene hardly to be surpassed.

The Jews have a custom singularly expressive and touching, one equally in harmony with the mournful associations which cluster around the holy city. At the foot of the western enclosure of the temple mount, where the walls tower to the height of sixty feet, are evident indications that the large stones at the base are the identical remains of the ancient wall of Solomon's temple. This portion of the wall they denominate the "mourning wall." It is visited by every Israelite on each feast and festival, and on every Friday afternoon. Here, in confident yet mournful expectation of again treading these courts of the Lord, which have so long been profaned by the foot of the Mussulman, the Jews reverentially bow their heads and repeat their wailings together in a most plaintive dirge, rehearsing various portions of their sacred psalms and prophetic lyrics expressive of their confiding lament: "How long yet, O Lord? O Lord our God, how long?"

57

THE TRAVELS OF OUR LORD.

We shall confine our attention to a few of the leading scenes of Christ's ministry, and try to throw upon his doings and discourses the light which is derived from the places and circumstances with which they are associated. The earlier and greater part of Christ's public ministry was exercised in the neighbourhood of the Sea of Galilee, as it was locally called; or, in the more correct language of the Gentile writer, Luke, the Lake of Gennesaret. The first of all His miracles was performed at a village called Cana, in Galilee (now a ruin), where, by turning water into wine, Christ seemed to indicate his power to sweeten and increase the comforts of human life. Crossing eastwards from the hills of Galilee, the traveller reaches a plain, called the Plain of Hattin. Here stands the hill commonly called the Mountain of Beatitudes, and said to be that from which the Sermon on the Mount was delivered. It is a square hill, not above sixty feet high, with two summits and a platform between them on which a multitude might find accommodation. From the top of this hill the Sea of Galilee is well seen. In Dr. Clarke's view, it is longer and finer than any of the lakes of Cumberland and Westmoreland, and only inferior to Loch Lomond in Scotland. In size, the lake is about thirteen miles long by six broad; but in the clearness of the Eastern atmosphere it looks smaller. What makes it unlike English lakes is its deep depression, which gives it something of the strange, unnatural character that belongs to the Dead Sea. On the east side the hills are flat, but on the north and west more varied and picturesque. Descending through the rocky walls which encompass it, the traveller meets with the thorn-tree and palm, and other products of a tropical climate. A strip of level, sandy beach surrounds the lake, from which the hills ascend, usually in gentle grassy slopes, broken by abrupt precipitous cliffs, the bright oleander and other plants often forming a pleasant fringe along the shore. On the western side an abundant supply of springs give birth to a verdure and fertility not found in the eastern.

At one part of the shore—at the northwest corner—the mountains recede, leaving a level, well-watered, fertile plain, five miles wide and six or seven long. This plain is the "land of Gennesaret," so closely identified with Christ's teaching and labors. Four springs pour their streams through it, magnificent cornfields show the riches of the soil, and along the shore a thick jungle of thorn and oleander affords a home to a multitude of birds. In the days of our Lord the plain of Gennesaret was crowded with cities and villages. Here stood Capernaum and Chorazin, one of the Bethsaidas, Magdala, and many other places, the very sites of which can hardly be distinguished. Besides land occupations, fishing was pursued with the greatest activity. The whole basin must have been a focus of life and energy—the surface of the lake constantly dotted with the white sails of vessels flying before the mountain gusts, as the beach sparkled with the houses and palaces, the synagogues and the temples of the Jewish or Roman inhabitants. It must have been an amazing contrast to the present deserted condition of the lake, where, in Dr. Robinson's time, a single boat was all that floated upon its waters.

An earnest spirit, like that of Jesus, toiling amid such a teeming population, and constantly filled with the sense of its spiritual miseries, could not obtain necessary rest or retirement, except by quitting the locality and getting into quite another scene. The mountains round the Lake of Gennesaret, especially those to the east, afforded to Jesus suitable and easily reached places of repose. He had but to retire a few miles from the shore, or to cross to the hills on the other side of the lake, to find a region as still and solitary as his usual residence was active and bustling. Hence the frequent references to "the mountains," where he spent nights in prayer; and to the "desert places," where he called his disciples to rest, on the other side of the lake. An hour's walk or sail would at any time transport Him from the bustle and strife of the streets of Capernaum to the stillest wilds of the desert.

It is to this spot, or its neighborhood, that we are to refer nearly all that is recorded of the life of Jesus to the end of the 18th chapter of Matthew. Yonder, a little way off, between the projecting "horns of Hattin," He delivered the Sermon on the Mount, encouraged the poor in spirit, taught His followers to pray "Our Father," and spoke of the broad road and the narrow way. The objects around supplied Him with natural and apt illustrations. The tulips and anemones on the plain below suggested the image of the "lilies of the field;" the numerous birds, in their bright and varied plumage, fluttering over the thickets near the lake, that of the "fowls of the air;" the fields, the rocks, the sea, and the desert, had all their part in the appeal, "What man is there of you, whom, if his son ask bread, will he give him a stone? or if he ask a fish, will he give him a serpent?" Perhaps the great crowded highway passing between the cities, contrasted with some lonely mountain-path, suggested the image of the broad and the narrow way; while some stable edifice built on the rock, and some slender shed by the sandy bed of a winter torrent, may have furnished the closing image of the wise and foolish builders.

Besides traversing several times the whole district of Galilee during His ministry, our Lord made some excursions to more distant places. On one of these occasions deeming it prudent, perhaps, to get beyond the jurisdiction of Herod, He came to the district of Phoenicia, "the coasts of Tyre and Sidon." Notwithstanding all the changes that had passed over it, Tyre

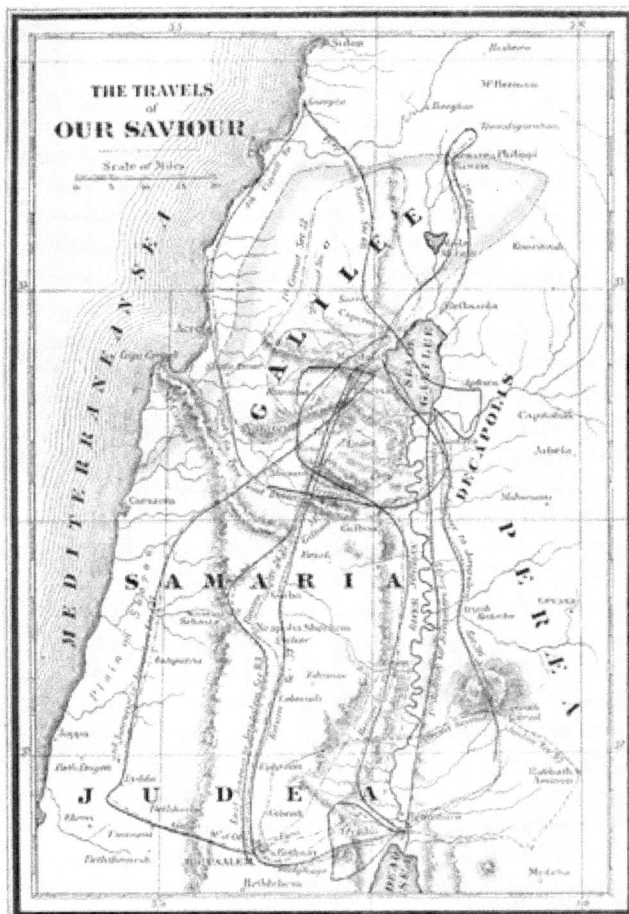

THE TRAVELS of OUR SAVIOUR

Scale of Miles

EXPLANATION OF MAP.

Because the Scriptural accounts of our Lord's travels are wanting in a careful mention of localities, this map must be rather more conjectural than the others. But though we may not now reach our information, such a sketch is valuable in impressing our minds as it does with his unwearying labors and wonderful devotion to his work of love.

There is, unavoidably, some confusion in such a chart; yet if attention is given to the different colors, this map will help us in following Him with reasonable correctness.

We have recognized the latest chronology in dating the dates four years before the common reckoning of the Christian era.

By this map we are shown our Saviour traversing the whole land: Judea, Samaria, and Galilee, from the wilderness on the south to the borders of Tyre, from the Mediterranean to the Jordan, everywhere in the fullest sympathy with the people; teaching them, reproving them, healing them, loving them divinely, by all means striving for their usefulness, and having compassion for their weakness and unbelief.

1. First, we may trace the earliest journey of Jesus to Jerusalem. In this journey he goes from Nazareth along the east side of Jordan to Bethabara, where he is baptized by John, and crossing, passes below Jericho, through the wilderness of Judea on to Jerusalem, a. d. 26. He returns through the wilderness to John at Bethabara, and thence upward to Cana and Capernaum, following the western bank of the river, passing Enon and Nazareth.

2. Jesus goes to Jerusalem a second time, by the western route, §21, a. d. 26. He followed in this journey the plains of Esdraelon and Sharon, and from Jerusalem we follow him to Enon, near Shalem, back to Jerusalem, thence toward Galilee by the middle route. In this journey we find him at Jacob's well, §23, and at Sychar, the Shechem of the Old Testament. He teaches in Galilee, §24, and returning by Cana and Nazareth, fixes his abode in Capernaum.

3. There can be no certainty about the first circuit in Galilee, a. d. 27, but it extended "throughout all Galilee" (Mark i. 39), and justified the indications of the map.

4. The third journey to Jerusalem, §26, a. d. 27, was along the table land east of Jordan, through Ramoth Gilead to the fords near Jericho. Returning, we follow him again along the middle line of travel, across the fertile plains of Mamre and Esdraelon, covered with fields of waving grain, where the disciples may have plucked the ears as they passed.

5. This is another purely conjectural circuit, around Upper Galilee, §47, a. d. 28.

6. The route indicates the excursion to the country of the Gadarenes, across the lake, §27, a. d. 27.

7. This is the third circuit in Galilee, §52, a. d. 28. It passes through Nazareth, Shunem, the plain of Esdraelon, and Tiberias. In this circuit the twelve were also sent to "supply his lack of service."

8. A trip to the northwest coast of the Sea of Galilee to Bethsaida, §56, a. d. 28.

9. The fourth circuit in Galilee, §61, a. d. 28. In this circuit Jesus passes over a wide range, through Sarepta, Tyre, Sidon, and the neighborhood of Decapolis beyond Jordan.

10. The fifth circuit in Galilee, §73, a. d. 28. He goes northeast of the Sea to Bethsaida and to Cesarea Philippi.

11. The fourth and final journey to Jerusalem, §91, a. d. 29, along the middle route, on which journey he cleansed the ten lepers of Samaria.

12. He makes a journey to Bethabara and returns to Bethany, called by the death of Lazarus, §11, a. d. 29.

Lastly, He makes the circuit to Ephraim, the valley of Jordan and Perea, §92, a. d. 29.

was still a strong citadel and a flourishing port; eclipsed partly by the Greek mercantile cities, but still carrying on much of that busy traffic which, in the days of the prophets, had made its merchants princes and its traffickers the honorable of the earth. Regarding Christ's emotions in connection with this remarkable country, we have but a single hint. He seems to have found a greater susceptibility to right impressions among the people there than in His own country; so that, when He reproved Chorazin and Bethsaida for their impenitence, He added the remarkable testimony, "If the mighty works which were done in you had been done in Tyre and Sidon, they would have repented long ago in sackcloth and ashes." The only incident recorded in connection with Christ's visit to this place is the cure of the daughter of the Syro-Phœnician woman. By His mercy to her He showed that even the once doomed and banned descendants of Canaan were not excluded from the sphere of His love and the reach of His blessings.

Another of Christ's more distant excursions was to the region of Cæsarea Philippi, near the sources of the Jordan. This Cæsarea was formerly called Paneas; it had just been repaired by the tetrarch Philip, and named Cæsarea after the emperor, Tiberius Cæsar, and Philippi after himself. It was situated at the foot of Mount Hermon, at the entrance to the noble valley between the ridges of Lebanon and Anti-Lebanon. It was but a few miles from Dan, the most northerly city of Palestine in former times, and the shrine of Jeroboam's idolatrous calves. When the Macedonians obtained possession of the country, they built at this place a shrine for Pan, the god of shepherds; whence the old name of the place, Paneas, and the present one, Banias, have come. In a precipitous face of the rock is a large dim grotto, with a niche, empty now, but formerly containing the statue of Pan; and other niches, which were the shrines of the nymphs.

It seems to have been during this visit to Cæsarea Philippi that the Transfiguration took place. And certainly the lofty summit of Hermon is far more likely to have been the scene of that wonderful event than the humble eminence of Mount Tabor. It is impossible to look up from the plain to the towering peaks of Hermon—almost the only mountain which deserves the name in Palestine—and not be struck with its appropriateness to the scene. That magnificent height, mingling with all the views of Palestine from Shechem upwards, though often alluded to as the northern barrier of the Holy Land, is connected with no historical event in the Old or New Testament. Yet this fact of its rising high above all the other hills of Palestine, and of its setting the last limit to the wanderings of Him who was sent only to the lost sheep of the house of Israel, falls in with the supposition which this words inevitably force on us. High up on its southern slopes there must be many a point where the disciples could be taken apart by themselves. Even the transient comparison of the celestial splendor with the snow, where alone it could be seen in Palestine, should not, perhaps, be wholly overlooked. At any rate, the remote heights above the sources of the Jordan witnessed the moment when—His work in His own peculiar sphere being ended—He set His face for the last time to go up to Jerusalem. During our Lord's residence at Capernaum, besides itinerating several times over Galilee, and making occasional excursions to more distant places, such as Sidon and Cæsarea, He went up, year by year, to Jerusalem, to attend the festivals. Both in going and returning "He must needs pass through Samaria," except when He preferred the route through the plain of Jordan, when Jericho would lie in His way. The most memorable occasion of His passing through Samaria was the time when He met with the woman at Jacob's well, near Sychar—the ancient Shechem.

The imagery of our Lord's teaching in Galilee had been drawn mainly from fishing and corn-fields. In Judea and the neighborhood of Jerusalem, vines and vineyards become the prominent figures. For still, as in the days of Isaiah, the "inhabitants of Jerusalem and the men of Judah," dwelling, as they did, "in a very fruitful hill," "binding their foal unto the vine and their ass's colt unto the choice vine," were most accessible to illustrations drawn from their staple employment. The parable of the laborers in the vineyard (Matt. xx. 1); that of the father and the two sons whom he sent to work in his vineyard (xxi. 28); that of the householder and the wicked husbandman to whom he let his vineyard (xxi. 33); and that of the true vine (John xv. 1), were all spoken either at Jerusalem or in its neighborhood. During the earlier visits of Christ to Jerusalem, He held His memorable conversation with Nicodemus; He cured the impotent man at the pool of Bethesda, and performed other miracles on the Sabbath; thereby shocking the prejudices of the Pharisees, and indicating the true character of the Sabbath as a day of blessing and privilege to man; He rescued and forgave the woman caught in adultery; welcomed publicans and sinners to salvation; and delivered the inimitable parables of the lost sheep, the lost piece of silver, and the prodigal son.

It was on occasion of His visits to Jerusalem that the loving heart of Jesus began to know, in all its depth of bitterness, the sensation of being hated, cursed, blasphemed. Each successive contest with the Scribes and Pharisees, ending, as it always did, in the triumph of Christ's superior meekness and wisdom, only added fuel to the burning fire of their jealousy. But now also, as He became familiar with the bitterness of human hatred, He came to know better the joys of holy human friendship. In the sequestered village of Bethany—an hour's walk from Jerusalem—Jesus had discovered the family most congenial with His own human heart. The holy fellowship enjoyed at night, under their humble cottage-roof, served to alleviate the pain arising from the conflicts of the day. It was not less as an endearing monument to the congenial spirit of that family than as a proof of His own power that Jesus, on one of His later visits, performed the stupendous miracle of raising Lazarus from the dead.

On occasion of the last visit our Lord paid to Jerusalem before His death, He travelled by Jericho. (Luke xviii. 31-35.) He had left Galilee a short time before, and spent the interval in Peræa, on the opposite side of the Jordan. The usual place for crossing the river below the Lake of Tiberias was the ford at Beth-shan, where the Philistines had fastened to the wall the bodies of Saul and his sons on the fatal day of Mount Gilboa; its ancient name had lately been exchanged for the Greek name Scythopolis, from an invasion of wild Scythian tribes that had taken place some time before. During His stay in Peræa, He seems to have stationed Himself near the spot where He had been baptized by John. This spot may have possessed peculiar charms for Him. It marked the beginning of His public life on earth. Here He had declared His purpose to fulfil all righteousness, and here He had received wonderful testimony from on high, and the singular anointing of the Holy Spirit, descending visibly upon Him; and from this spot His eye wandered over other places sacred to scenes full of precious significance. Among other memorable incidents that occurred here was the conversation with the mother of James and John about the chief places of honor in His kingdom. Close to this place, on the dark mountain-wall of Moab, was the height on which Moses yielded his spirit into the hands of God, and also the spot where the chariot of fire and horses of fire came for Elijah. Under thoughts of His own coming death-struggle, it would soothe Jesus to remember the words and tones in which these two prophets, a short time before, on the snowy heights of Mount Hermon, had prepared His mind for the defence which He was about to accomplish at Jerusalem.

At last the Passover drawing nigh, He and His disciples re-cross the Jordan, near the place where Joshua and the host of Israel had crossed it, and come to Jericho with its palm groves and fountains. The fame of Jesus has reached the place, and a great multitude has turned out to see Him. Two blind men by the wayside have raised their imploring voices, have received mercy, and are now feasting their wondering eyes on the glories of nature. Aloft on the sycamore-tree Zacchæus, the rich publican, has taken his place, forgetful of his dignity in his eagerness to get a glimpse of the great Galilean, and little thinking how much closer fellowship he is that day to have with Him—how he is to give Him a twofold welcome as a guest in his house, and as a Saviour in his heart. The eagerness of Christian faith always lays a double offering on the altar of the Saviour. With the ardor of love is the earnestness of service. The delight of receiving Jesus is the declaration of self-renouncement. "O Christ! I accept Thee! O Christ, accept me!" are the confession and prayer of the penitent.

Leaving Jericho, Jesus proceeds on His way, repeating to His audience the parable of the pounds, so forcibly conveying the great lessons of accountability which enter so vitally into all our relations, that parable which clothes the smallest advantage, the most inconsiderable capacity with all the solemnity of a divine gift in sacred trust. Climbing the steep mountain-passes, He traverses the scene of the parable of the good Samaritan, in which He impresses on human hearts the wonderful kindness of His own, and lifts their souls toward a realm of sympathy and tenderness more Divine than human, while He shows them the golden chain of brotherly obligation in which He binds His people; at last He reaches the village of Bethany, where sweet thoughts of former times throng upon Him, and every bough and bird and blossom tell of friends eager always with their love and hospitality—where lingers yet the memory of His mighty power over death and tearful affection. Proceeding next day to Jerusalem, He is met by the great crowd from the city that have heard of His arrival, and rides in triumph over the palm-spread road—an accurate fulfilment of the words pronounced by Zechariah more than five hundred years before; a singular triumph over the fears and prejudices of the people, which were soon again to arise and break forth in cruel denials and heartless accusations. The path leads first up the eastern side of Olivet, then down to Jerusalem on the west. As it passes over the ridge, Jerusalem suddenly bursts on the view like a thing of enchantment. Beholding the beloved city, the Saviour wept over it, and poured out His whole heart in the memorable lament: "If thou hadst known, even thou, at least in this thy day, the things which belong unto thy peace! but now they are hid from thine eyes."

Of the localities in the immediate neighborhood of Jerusalem specially consecrated by the footsteps of Jesus, the Mount of Olives and the Garden of Gethsemane hold very distinguished places. The Mount of Olives is a long low ridge extending along the east side of the city, with three several summits. Its name was derived from the olive groves that probably flourished at one time in far greater luxuriance than now; for it is only in one of the slopes that anything like an olive forest can now be seen, although scattering trees appear elsewhere. At the Jerusalem foot of Olivet, close to the brook Kidron and the valley of Jehoshaphat, lies the Garden of Gethsemane. It is a square of about 150 feet. "When we saw it in May," says Lieutenant Lynch, "the trees were in full bloom; and altogether the garden, in its aspects and associations, was better calculated than any place I know to soothe a troubled spirit. Eight venerable trees, isolated from the smaller and less imposing ones which skirt the pass of the Mount of Olives, form a consecrated grove, whose deep shadows blending darkly entertain our meditations of the scene of anguish. It seems a fitting sanctuary for such sorrow. It reminds us of the sequestered walks of the garden which were all radiant with the brightness of love divine until the brow of God darkened on man's sin. In this darkened bower Christ suffered in redemption of the Paradise lost by man."

The Son of man had now all but accomplished the work given Him to do. He had shown a spotless example of all excellence as a man; and in that holy human life had exhibited the image of the invisible God. He had established His claims to the Messiahship, had fulfilled Old Testament prophecies and types, wrought miracles, performed acts of beneficence, and uttered words of divine power and sweetness that showed clearly that He came from God. He had vindicated the law and the prophets from the perversions of the rabbins; had demonstrated that all true goodness must come from the heart; had shown that a renewed will and a pure life are the only real evidence of a right state with God; and had denounced, in withering words that could never be forgotten, the hollow hypocrisy and pretentious formality of the leading religionists of the day. He had shown that a spiritual homage is the only acceptable worship of God; and had encouraged His followers to render that worship by revealing God's fatherly character and great love even for his lost and fallen children. While thus raising the standard of holy living, He had revealed Himself in His divine nature as the Life of men; and under such emblems as the Living Bread, the Living Water, and the True Vine, had taught them where to find the inward strength required for their duty. In His conversation with Nicodemus—one of the earliest on record—He had unfolded the grand gospel doctrines: Ruin by Sin, Regeneration by the Holy Spirit, and Reconciliation by the sacrifice of Himself. It now only remained, by His sacrifice on the cross, to complete that redemption which Messiah was to achieve; to grapple with the last enemy, and by conquering Death show clearly that He was, as He had said, the Resurrection and the Life.

It is the last evening of His mortal life. Night has now fallen, and the Master and His little band seek quiet beyond the walls of the crowded city. They have passed the brook Kidron; eight of them linger in the valley, while Peter, James and John accompany Him into Gethsemane. Stretched on the bare ground, under the gnarled and twisted olives, the struggle of His great agony comes on. Not even that heavenly Helper, whose white form the disciples see gliding through the gloom of the night, has been able to remove His terror. He who has so often said, "Fear not," now seems given up to fear. But at last tranquillity returns. And now the glare of torches is seen across the Kidron. Nearer the din of rough voices is heard. With noisy progress they make straight for Gethsemane, for Judas knows the place. The traitor's kiss is given to the Saviour; He surrenders Himself without resistance; His disciples fly; alone and helpless He goes back a prisoner to the city. He is conducted to the house of Annas, who sends Him bound to Caiaphas. In his palace the rest of the night is spent. Early next day the Sanhedrim assemble, with the chief priests and scribes, and find Jesus guilty of a capital offence. But they have not the power of inflicting death; the Roman governor must therefore confirm their sentence, so they lead Him to the Praetorium, or judgment-hall of Pilate. An unexpected obstacle to their scheme here presents itself. The unscrupu-

lous Roman governor has become strangely scrupulous, and is most unwilling to condemn this extraordinary Prisoner. As the day wears on, he occupies hour after hour in attempts to release Him; for a strange impression has laid hold of him that this Jesus is not an ordinary criminal, and that to give Him up to death would be an unpardonable crime. Hearing that He is a Galilean, he sends Him to Herod, who is at Jerusalem attending the feast; and Herod, after examining Him, sends Him back to the perplexed and hesitating Pilate. But at last a skilful appeal to the fears of the governor settles the question. He knows how precarious is his hold of office; and when the cry gets up, "If thou let this man go, thou art not Caesar's friend," he has no longer courage to resist. Jesus is delivered to be crucified, and is led away to Calvary. At Calvary, or rather Golgotha, the Roman punishment of crucifixion is inflicted on Him. The typical prophecy of the brazen serpent—"lifted up"—is fulfilled, as well as that of the paschal lamb—"a bone of Him shall not be broken." Had the Jewish punishment of stoning been inflicted, such would not have been the case. Over His head the words, "Jesus of Nazareth, the King of the Jews," are placed, in Hebrew, Greek and Latin; for all three languages are now spoken in Jerusalem. After hours of protracted misery the sufferings of Jesus come at last to an end. The Prince of Life bows His head and gives up the ghost. Joseph of Arimathea, a member of the Sanhedrim, goes to Pilate and begs the body; and Nicodemus brings a great load of myrrh and aloes, and wraps them in a linen cloth around the corpse. As the hour of sunset, when the Jewish Sabbath commenced, is now drawing on, the body is hastily placed in Joseph's tomb, in the adjacent garden. And Jesus, having finished the great work of Redemption, rests in His grave till the morning of the third day.

The next day is the Sabbath. It brings no relief to the staggering faith of the disciples. This whole day Jesus rests in the sepulchre. But the early light of the following morning shows His empty tomb, and the risen Saviour reveals Himself to some of His apostles and followers. One week after He shows Himself to them again at Jerusalem, and rebukes and removes the unbelief of Thomas. A mountain in Galilee having been appointed as a place of meeting, the apostles return to their native province. There, first on the shore of the lake so familiar to them all, He joins the eleven, dines with them on part of the miraculous draught of fishes, and puts to Peter the threefold question, "Lovest thou Me?" Afterwards, on the appointed mountain, He shows Himself to all His Galilean disciples, upwards of five hundred in number. Last of all, He again meets the eleven at Jerusalem; and when He had crossed for the last time the Mount of Olives, and come to the well-known village of Bethany, it came to pass, that, as He blessed them, He was parted from them, and a cloud received Him out of their sight. His work on earth was done; and the crucified outcast of Galilee "forever sat down on the right hand of God."

THE TRAVELS OF ST. PAUL.

The missionary labors of Paul occupied a period of thirty-five years, from A. D. 33 to 68. They began at Damascus, where, upon his conversion, Paul straightway in the synagogues preached that Jesus was the Son of God. After a few days he went out into unknown regions of Arabia, in fulfilment of his apostolic mission. Then, returning to Damascus, he narrowly escaped assassination, and went from there to Jerusalem. Finding himself distrusted by the Christians, whom he had formerly persecuted, he retired to Tarsus, his native city, in Cilicia. Here he remained in obscurity till Barnabas came for him and took him to Antioch to assist in a revival there. This city for "a whole year" was the scene of Paul's ministry, and for many years the centre of his missionary operations. Embarking at Seleucia, Paul went with Barnabas to the island of Cyprus. At the two extremities of the island, Salamis and Paphos, the gospel was preached; and at the latter place, Sergius Paulus, the Roman governor, became a convert. A Jewish sorcerer named Bar-Jesus, or, in Greek, Elymas, made a vehement effort to withstand the apostles, and prevent the conversion of the governor. The contest with this sorcerer was Paul's first great battle. Full of faith and power, he rebuked his countryman in language of stunning intensity, and brought temporary blindness upon him. The effect on the mind of the governor was favorable; he became a firm believer.

Sailing from Cyprus, the apostles returned to the mainland, crossing the Pamphylian gulf, and going first to Perga, the chief town of Pamphylia. Here, Mark, who had accompanied them hitherto, frightened probably in a moment of weak faith, when he learned that Paul and Barnabas meant to penetrate into the wilds of Pisidia, left them and returned to Jerusalem. At Perga they did not remain long, but climbing the mountain-passes that separate Pamphylia from the table-land or elevated plain of Pisidia, reached Antioch, a city which was as much Roman in its composition as Perga was Greek. A commotion was raised, and the apostles had to quit the Pisidian Antioch, shaking the dust from their feet against their countrymen. Proceeding about ninety miles in an easterly direction, the apostles came to Iconium. This town, afterwards called Konieh, became celebrated in history as the cradle of the rising power of the conquering Turks. The elements of its population would be as follows: a large number of frivolous Greeks; some remains of a still older population; a few Roman officials; and an old colony of Jews. The same treatment was given to the apostles here as at Antioch, and they fled to the more rural villages of Derbe and Lystra. At Lystra the miraculous cure of a lame man caused them to be mistaken for Jupiter and Mercury. The fickle multitude, who had first proposed to worship the apostles, being stirred up by the Jews from

Antioch and Iconium, ended by stoning them. Paul was so hurt that he was left for dead.

They now retraced their steps, and returned to confirm and comfort the churches which they had planted, amid the persecutions against which they had to struggle. The only new place they are said to have visited was Attalia, on the sea-coast of Pamphylia. From that port they sailed to the Syrian Antioch, where they rehearsed to the brethren the tidings of the success of the gospel among the Gentiles. It was resolved by the brethren at Antioch to send Paul and Barnabas and others to Jerusalem. In the course of their journey, the apostles passed through Phœnicia and Samaria, where the gospel had made great progress, and where many hearts were made glad by the tidings which they carried. At last they reached Jerusalem. It was now fifteen years since Paul's conversion, and fourteen since the first visit he had paid as a Christian to that city. The assembly was addressed by Peter, Paul, Barnabas and James. After the council, Paul and Barnabas returned to Antioch, accompanied by Barnabas and Silas. Paul proposed to Barnabas that they should make a tour of inspection, visiting and watering the churches which they had formerly planted. An unhappy quarrel took place between them, occasioned by the desire of Barnabas to take his nephew Mark along with them, and Paul's want of thorough confidence in Mark, caused by his having left them in Pamphylia. As the two apostles could not agree, they took separate routes, Barnabas and Mark going to Cyprus, while Paul, accompanied by Silas, traversed a large portion of the provinces of Asia Minor.

The first visits of Paul and Silas were paid to the districts of Syria and Cilicia, the provinces where Paul had labored and preached the gospel soon after his conversion. Doubtless his native Tarsus was among the places which he now visited; but no details have been preserved of his actings there. Next, striking up in a northwesterly course, through one of the "gates" or passes of the Taurus, he returned to Derbe and Lystra. Great must have been his joy to find his young friend Timothy so strong in the grace that is in Christ Jesus, and so well reported of by the brethren both at Lystra and Iconium. It would be with mingled emotions of joy and sorrow that his grandmother and mother saw Timothy depart with Paul and Silas. Striking into galatia, Paul entered on new ground, and came among quite a new race. The Galatians, as the first syllable of their name implies, were of Gallic origin; four centuries before their ancestors had worshipped under the oaks of Gaul. They had been borne along in an emigration that at last brought them from the west of Europe to the west of Asia.

After traversing Phrygia and Galatia, it would have been

22

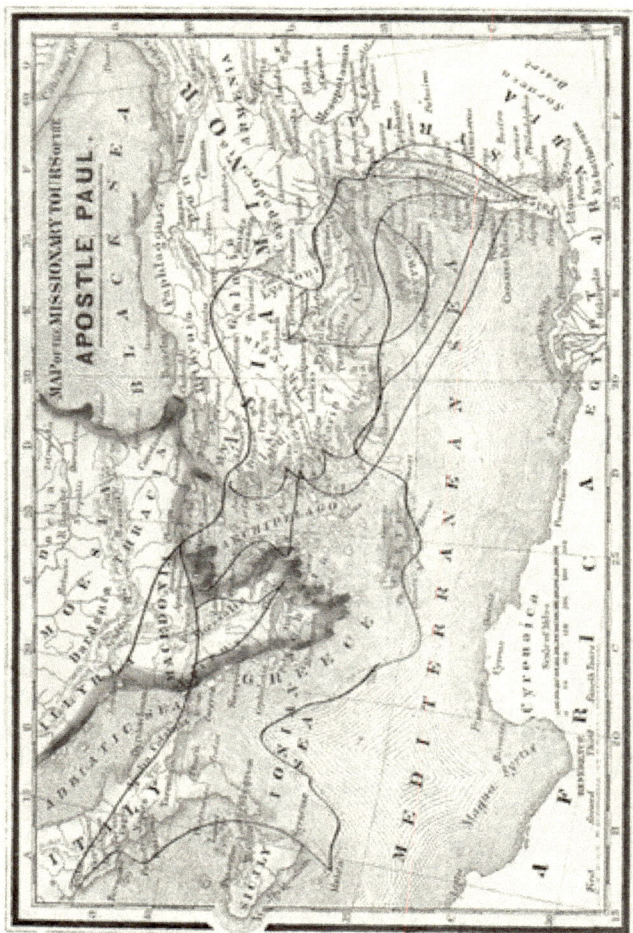

MAP of the MISSIONARY TOURS of the APOSTLE PAUL

EXPLANATION OF MAP.

This map is entitled to the highest confidence; it was prepared in the first place for "Coneybeare's History of the Christian Church," in the time of the Apostles. It was constructed according to the latest researches from the beautiful classical maps of Greece and Asia Minor, and its own learning put it in its present form. It is sustained by the series of splendid maps to be found in the great work on the life of St. Paul by Coneybeare and Howson.

1. The Apostle Paul goes to Jerusalem for the first time from Damascus. It is after his conversion. He is supposed to sail from Cæsarea for Tarsus, A. D. 38.

2. Paul is invited by Barnabas to Antioch, A. D. 44, and on the occasion of the famine, visits Jerusalem the second time in company with Barnabas, A. D. 45. We cannot obtain accuracy for the route as indicated, but they are thought to have passed the Orontes and Cœle-Syria, and to have returned to Joppa by sea.

3. There is no conjecture about this first missionary tour of the Apostle through Cyprus and Pamphylia to Antioch in Pisidia, Iconium, Lystra, and Derbe in Lycaonia, and back again by the same route to Perga, Attalia, and Antioch.

4. The third time Paul goes to Jerusalem to the great council about circumcision; he was accompanied by Barnabas and Titus. (See Gal. ii. 1.) Through the mediation of Jerusalem, they passed along the great Roman road down the Phœnician coast. Returning, they passed through Damascus on to Antioch, A. D. 50.

5. This shows the second missionary tour of Paul, in which he visits Troas by land, and goes on to Derbe, Lystra, Iconium, through Galatia and Phrygia to Troas, A. D. 52. He visits Macedonia, Athens, Corinth, Ephesus, Cæsarea, and Jerusalem the fourth time, A. D. 54.

6. The third missionary tour of Paul, which brings him to Jerusalem the fifth and last time, passes through Ephesus, Galatia, and Pamphylia, where he strengthened the churches, through Ephesus and Macedonia to Corinth. From Corinth, returning, he passes through Thessaly to Philippi, thence to Miletus and Tyre, and to Jerusalem.

7. We may trace very distinctly the voyage to Rome in the autumn and winter of A. D. 60-61. From Cæsarea he passed up the coast around Cyprus, thence along the coast road of Asia Minor to Cnidus, thence following the southern route of Crete to Melita and Syracuse, through the Straits of Sicily to the Bay of Naples, and along this Appian Way through the Pontine Marshes to Rome.

natural for Paul to direct his course to the great seaport of Ephesus, but "they were forbidden by the Holy Ghost to preach the word in Asia." Bithynia, too, seemed closed against them. The only district to which they had access was Troas, which still preserved the immortal name of Troy. In a vision Paul heard a voice saying, "Come over into Macedonia and help us." That cry of distress was not to be disregarded. Next morning Paul and his companions, of whom the beloved physician Luke was now one, might be seen on the quay of Troas, eagerly inquiring for the first ship to Macedonia. The wind wafts them through the seas that bore, 500 years before, the magnificent armada of Xerxes. The story of the shepherd's sling and stone is again about to be realised. These four humble men in the Trojan ship are to accomplish what the millions of Xerxes failed to accomplish—conquer Greece and Europe too. The first campaign of the gospel of Jesus Christ in Europe was fought in Macedonia; Philippi, Thessalonica, and Berea were the principal battle-fields. A woman in middle life, the head of a house—a girl possessed by a demon—and a cruel jailer, were among the persons first struck down at Philippi by the arrows of the King.

From Philippi the apostle proceeded to Thessalonica, an important seaport, with a Jewish synagogue. From this busy place the holy fame of the new religion, which was embraced by many of the old Pagans, sounded out through all the neighboring districts of Macedonia on the north and Achaia on the south. But persecution drove Paul from Thessalonica, as it had driven him from Philippi. He took refuge in the provincial town of Berea, where, through the diligent study of the Scriptures, many Jews were converted, and also some of the principal Gentiles. The signs of another gathering storm led the brethren in haste to send Paul away, while Silas and Timothy remained at Berea. A ship bound for Athens conveyed the apostle from the shore, where Olympus, dark with woods, rises from the plain to the broad summit glittering with snow, which was the home of the Homeric gods. On three different spots Paul bore testimony to the truth at Athens. The first was the synagogue of the Jews; the next was a more public platform—the Agora or market-place—the common meeting-place of the Athenians. Some of the philosophers who heard Paul here, wishing to listen to him in a quieter and more solemn place, took him to Areopagus, or Mars' Hill. Here he summoned the proud and haughty Stoic to repent of all his wickedness, and foretold the coming of a terrible day of retribution by God's Son; of which the certain pledge had been given to all men, in that he had raised him from the dead.

Paul had paid his visit to Athens alone; but at Corinth, to which he next proceeded, he was joined by Silas and Timothy. Here Paul had great success. Crispus, the ruler of a synagogue, became a convert—a circumstance that must have caused great excitement. Yet Paul's spirit was

burdened and depressed. That which distressed him was the bitter and blasphemous opposition to the truth which the Jews were ever exciting. But the Lord mercifully encouraged him in a vision, and for a year and a half he continued to labor at Corinth. It was now that he wrote his two epistles to the Thessalonians—the earliest of all his recorded letters. At last, having a strong desire to be present at one of the festivals at Jerusalem, he set sail for the holy city, taking Ephesus on his way. Promising to try to return to Ephesus, he went on to Jerusalem, and after his visit returned to Antioch, thus completing his second great missionary tour.

The third missionary campaign of the apostle, during all of which he had Timothy for his companion, opened in Phrygia and Galatia, where he had been before. But the chief place to which his attention was directed in this tour was Ephesus. Sorcery or magic—an importation of the East—was exceedingly common. Diana, a goddess of the West, was the great object of worship; but the style of worship had in it much of oriental mystery and magnificence. On leaving Ephesus, Paul first went to Troas, where he preached with great success; then proceeded to Macedonia and the countries of Greece lying to the north. He seems at this time to have been in a dejected state of mind. At Philippi he wrote the Second Epistle to the Corinthians. He was now actively engaged in a scheme for collecting money for the poor believers in Judea, designed to show the good-will of the Gentiles, and to soften down the bitter feeling of the Jewish Church towards their uncircumcised brethren. Three months were then spent in Corinth; and the Epistle to the Romans was written, and despatched by Phebe.

Leaving Europe, Paul now directed his course to Jerusalem. He proceeded by sea, and his voyage was full of interest. After spending a week at Troas, taking a most affectionate farewell of the Ephesian Christians at Miletus, and touching at Coos, Rhodes and Patara, the apostle and his companions sailed to Tyre. A church had existed there since the persecution at the death of Stephen, and there were now not only Christians but prophets in what had once been a great stronghold of Baal and Ashtaroth. Leaving Tyre, the party saluted the brethren at Ptolemais, and at length reached Cæsarea. From that place, in opposition to the remonstrances of the Evangelist Philip and other friends, who dreaded the excited feelings of the Jews, Paul travelled to Jerusalem, where he was received kindly by James and the elders, and refreshed them by telling what God had been doing among the Gentiles.

We can only refer in general terms to the occurrences that took place while Paul was in Palestine. The hatred towards him of that part of the Church which was leavened with the spirit of the Pharisees found a speedy outlet. On a false clamor being raised, he was beaten by the people in the temple; rescued, however, by the Roman soldiers, and carried to the neighboring fort and barrack of Antonia; there he was about to be put on the rack, but escaped the torture by declaring himself a Roman citizen; was tried before the Sanhedrim, as Stephen had been twenty-five years before, when he was himself a virulent persecutor; received in a vision a cheering promise of protection from God; and a plot against his life being discovered, was sent, with a large escort, by night, to the Roman capital, Cæsarea. The Roman governor, resident at Cæsarea at this time, was Claudius Felix, an unscrupulous, sensual profligate, whose wife Drusilla was a daughter of Herod Agrippa I. On his first appearance before Felix, Paul was remanded, under pretense of being tried again; the next time, in presence of Drusilla, he made Felix tremble, as he reasoned of righteousness, temperance, and judgment to come; after that he was kept a prisoner at Cæsarea for two years. At the end of that period Felix was recalled from Palestine, and Porcius Festus sent as governor in his room. Paul was now tried again, and on this occasion took his memorable appeal to Cæsar.

The record of Paul's voyage to Rome, in the twenty-seventh chapter of Acts, is remarkably interesting. The vessel, on leaving the great dock constructed by Herod at Cæsarea, touched at Sidon; then passing to the north of Cyprus, through the Gulfs of Cilicia and Pamphylia, afforded the apostle a view, probably his last, of his native mountains. At Myra, in Lycia, a ship was found chartered for Rome, to which the prisoners were transferred. After creeping along slowly as far as Cnidus, adverse winds forced the ship out of her direct course, compelling her to pass southward, under lee of the island of Crete, as far as the harbor called Fair Havens. After waiting long for a favorable breeze, the vessel set sail, but had not proceeded far when she was caught by a furious gale from the northeast. The crew seem to have turned round the right side of the vessel to the wind, and allowed her to be carried along, on the starboard tack, in a westerly direction. In the circumstances it is reckoned that she would drift at the rate of about a mile and a half in the hour. After a fortnight of discomfort and terror that can hardly be conceived, the sailors became sensible, one midnight, that they were approaching land. The ship was immediately anchored astern, and daylight anxiously waited for. When it came, it was observed that a creek ran into the shore. Into this creek the vessel was attempted to be run; but in the attempt her bow stuck fast in the bottom. Partly by swimming, and partly through the aid of boards and broken pieces of the ship, all the passengers, who were two hundred and seventy-six in number, got safely to land.

The island on which the ship was cast was Malta, now a part of the British possessions. The bay where the shipwreck occurred still bears the name of St. Paul; and all the circumstances of the shipwreck, as recorded in the Acts, agree wonderfully with existing appearances. The island was inhabited by a people of Phœnician origin. After spending three months among them, Paul and his companions embarked in another vessel; touched at Syracuse in Sicily;

had to wait at Rhegium for a favorable wind to carry them through the Straits of Messina; and at last, after gazing on the smoking crater of Vesuvius and the lovely scenery of the Bay of Naples, landed at Puteoli. From this seaport to Rome, a distance of 130 miles, the apostle travelled by land. At Appii Forum, 50 miles from Rome, and again at the Three Taverns, deputations from the Christians of the city came to offer to the great apostle of the Gentiles the expression of their deep regard and affection. For two years he continued a prisoner, dwelling in his own lodging, but constantly chained to a Roman soldier. At last his trial came on; most probably it was conducted in the immediate presence of Nero. It is from Paul's epistles we learn that he was set free.

It is generally believed that from Rome he went to Asia Minor, and from that to Macedonia. He seems then to have gone to Spain, where he is thought to have spent two years. Returning to Ephesus, he found matters in a somewhat critical condition. In Crete, too, which he visited about this time, he found much cause for anxiety. False teachers were busy perverting the truth and sapping the foundations of Christianity. Paul had hoped to spend the winter at Nicopolis, in Macedonia; but he was not allowed to remain there. He was arrested on a new charge, and hurried to Rome to stand a second trial. Since he had been last at Rome, Nero had conducted himself in a very shameful way. More than half the city had been burned by an awful fire, which lasted for six days, and which some ascribe to Nero himself. The blame was laid by him upon the Christians, who were now an exceedingly numerous body. A frightful persecution raged against them. Some were crucified; some disguised in the skins of beasts, and hunted to death with dogs; some were wrapped in robes impregnated with inflammable materials, and set on fire at night, that they might serve to illuminate the circus of the Vatican and the gardens of Nero, where this diabolical monster exhibited the agonies of his victims to the public, and gloated over them. The number who perished was very great. Paul's privileges on his second confinement seem to have been much smaller than on his first. The Second Epistle to Timothy was now written by him, in the full expectation of being offered up. When brought to trial, in presence of a large number of leading men, he was enabled to make a bold statement of the gospel. But no defence could avail against the will of Nero. The apostle, on being called a second time, was condemned. Near the spot now occupied by the English cemetery, his head was struck from his body. Devout men carried the headless corpse to the catacombs, or subterranean vaults below Rome, to which in after times the martyrs used often to fly for concealment. There, in some unknown vault, rests the body of the greatest of the apostles, awaiting the fulfilment of the words so nobly applied by himself—"Death shall be swallowed up in victory."

ANCIENT JERUSALEM

MODERN JERUSALEM

MODERN JERUSALEM

I. THE CHRISTIAN QUARTER.

1. Golgotha's Castle.
2. Latin Convent.
3. Church of the Holy Sepulchre.
4. Greek Convent.
5. Coptic Convent.
6. House of St. John's Hospital.
7. Greek Church, St. John's.
8. Residence of the Christian Bishop.
9. Church of the Greek Schismatics.
10. Tower of Hippicus. David's Tower.
11. Supposed site of the Tower of Phasælus.
12. The Piscina Gennath.
13. Nestorian Ethiopian Church.
14. Hospital and Syrian Convent.

II. THE ARMENIAN QUARTER.

15. Armenian Convent, with the Church of St. James.
    The only building in Jerusalem which presents any appearance of neatness.
16. Nunnery of St. George.
17. Barracks.

III. THE JEWS' QUARTER.

For most crowded in the city.

18. Synagogue of the Sephardim.
19. Synagogue of the Portuguese Jews.
20. Mosque.

IV. THE MOHAMMEDAN QUARTER.

21. Khan and Bazaar.
22. Mineral Bath.
23. Fountain and Schools.
24. Basilica for Sifted Dervishes.

25. Hospital of St. Helen.
26. Reputed site of the House of the Rich Man.
27. Reputed site of the House of St. Veronica.
28. Residence of the Turkish Pasha.
29. Arch of the "Ecce Homo."
30. Point of the "Black Stone," the Holy Sakhrain.
31. Pilate's House.
32. Place of Flagellation.
33. Ruins of a Church. House of Simon the Pharisee.
34. Church of St. Anne.
35. House of Herod. Bevish's Mosque.

V. THE MOORS' QUARTER.

a. Armenian Convent. House of Caiaphas.
b. Armenian Burial-ground.
c. David's Tomb.
d. Place of Wailing of the Jews.

Just outside Zion's Gate are the scattered abodes of lepers.

www.ingramcontent.com/pod-product-compliance
Lightning Source LLC
Chambersburg PA
CBHW032144080426
42733CB00008B/1194